21 THIN
YOU WON'T
LEARN IN
ARCHITECTURE
SCHOOL

21 Things You Won't Learn in Architecture School

© Adrian Dobson, 2014

Published by RIBA Publishing, part of RIBA Enterprises Ltd,
The Old Post Office, St Nicholas Street, Newcastle upon Tyne, NE1 1RH

ISBN 9781859465677

Stock code 82662

British Library Cataloguing in Publications Data
A catalogue record for this book is available from the British Library.

Image credits
Allford Hall Monaghan Morris Ltd 74, 79
Bob Allies 107
John Assael 94, 99
Caroline Buckingham 118, 123
Adrian Dobson xi, 160
Shankari Raj Edgar 148, 153
Hyde + Hyde 80, 85
Soraya Khan 159
Marianne Davys Architects 102
David Partridge 140, 145
Penoyre & Prasad 86, 92
Satwinder Samra 132, 138
Neringa Stonyte 124
Philip Vile 154
xsite architecture LLP 129
Zedfactory 110, 115

Publisher: Steven Cross
Commissioning Editor: Sarah Busby
Project Editor: Richard Blackburn
Designed by Kneath Associates
Typeset by Academic & Technical, Bristol
Printed and bound by W&G Baird Ltd in Great Britain

RIBA Publishing is part of RIBA Enterprises Ltd.
www.ribaenterprises.com

CONTENTS

Foreword		vii
About the author		viii
Acknowledgements		viii
Why you should read this book		ix

PART 1	21 Things You Won't Learn in Architecture School	03
	01 In architecture, it's a long road to success	05
	02 There is more than one type of successful architect	09
	03 Architectural practices come in many forms	13
	04 Architecture doesn't exist in a vacuum	15
	05 You need to develop interests beyond architecture	19
	06 Architects think differently	21
	07 Speak in a language your audience understands	25
	08 Architects always work in teams	29
	09 Teams need leaders	33
	10 Architecture is a business	37
	11 Architects can learn business skills	41
	12 Architects have to sell and negotiate	43
	13 Work out what kind of architect you want to be and play to your strengths	47
	14 Communicate your unique message	49
	15 You need to understand fees	51
	16 Focus on people and process, not product	57
	17 Keep up to date with new technology and new thinking	61
	18 Look after your personal brand and networks	65
	19 Prizes matter – don't they?	67
	20 Construction sometimes involves conflict as well as collaboration	69
	21 There is no architecture without design	71

PART 2   The Interviews   73

    01   Simon Allford, *Allford Hall Monaghan Morris*   75

    02   Kay Hyde, *Hyde + Hyde Architects*   81

    03   Sunand Prasad, *Penoyre and Prasad*   87

    04   John Assael, *Assael Architecture*   95

    05   Marianne Davys, *Marianne Davys Achitects*   103

    06   Bill Dunster, *ZEDfactory*   111

    07   Caroline Buckingham, *HLM Architects*   119

    08   Tim Bailey, *xsite architecture*   125

    09   Satwinder Samra, *School of Architecture,
       University of Sheffield*   133

    10   David Partridge, *Argent*   141

    11   Shankari Raj Edgar, *Nudge Group*   149

    12   Soraya Khan, *Theis and Khan Architects*   155

Adfyd a ddwg wybodaeth, a gwybodaeth ddoethineb.
Adversity brings knowledge, and knowledge wisdom.

(Welsh proverb)

FOREWORD

Anyone about to embark on an architectural education knows one thing for certain – it'll be at least seven years before you can even call yourself an architect. It's the first thing you're told when you sign up. In fact it seems to be the first thing anyone ever says when you mention you're an architecture student. But what happens when you've got your Part 3? Surely there must be something someone can tell you about what it's like to actually *be* an architect, right?

As someone who got about halfway through training before sidling off into journalism, I can say quite confidently that I didn't know much about the industry before signing up. Apart from being told, "it's not all fancy museums and beautiful houses", I didn't have any idea what to expect from working in practice. From how much I would be likely to earn, to what kind of architect I wanted to be, or what firm I might end up in. For some reason, when it comes to architecture, we all seem to forget about the practicalities and jump in with both feet. It may be because students are encouraged to think of architecture as some kind of passion that we all forget to ask what the job actually involves. Maybe it's because we're happy to accept any conditions, as long as we get to take the credit for beautiful buildings. Who knows?

Luckily, this book sets out to put an end to that, with a handy list of 21 things that seem obvious, but that most architecture graduates, like me, never actually thought about for the largest part of that gruelling seven-year stint. It's filled with practical pieces of advice that encompass everything from understanding fee scales and team structures, to avoiding words like "juxtaposition" and "axis". Most of all, it's a guide to what working in architecture is *really* like, and how to get the best from it.

It's about time architectural practice became a little bit more transparent and luckily, with this book, it does.

Amy Frearson
Deputy Editor, Dezeen

ABOUT THE AUTHOR

Adrian Dobson is Director of Practice at the Royal Institute of British Architects. He is a Chartered Architect with practice experience primarily in the education and community sectors. He has also taught in higher education and carried out research in building information modelling.

As RIBA Director of Practice, Adrian has been at the forefront of the launch of the new RIBA Plan of Work 2013, the key design and construction process map used throughout the construction industry. He has also been closely involved in supporting authors in the development of core RIBA practice publications including the *RIBA Job Book*, the *RIBA Handbook of Practice Management*, the *RIBA Agreements* and *A Client's guide to Engaging an Architect*.

ACKNOWLEDGEMENTS

I would like to acknowledge the support of the 12 architects who so generously agreed to be interviewed for this book. Thank you to Simon Allford, John Assael, Tim Bailey, Caroline Buckingham, Marianne Davys, Bill Dunster, Shankari Edgar, Kay Hyde, Soraya Khan, David Partridge, Sunand Prasad and Satwinder Samra. The insights provided by this daring dozen were essential to the realisation of the project, and a source of inspiration to me both personally and professionally.

I would also like to thank Sarah Busby, Commissioning Editor at RIBA Publications, for her help in developing the concept and ideas for this publication, and her patience and fortitude in ensuring that time, cost and, I hope, quality targets were met.

WHY YOU SHOULD READ THIS BOOK

Few people commence a career in architecture with the primary aim of achieving rich financial rewards; there are probably better options available if that is your main goal. The more ego-driven may be motivated by the desire to leave behind some form of permanent imprint for posterity. Some perhaps fall into it as an acceptable alternative to apparently more mundane, less creative, traditional professional occupations. But it is my belief that most become architects because they have a passion to create a better world for people through contributing to making the best possible built environment in which to live, work and play.

Many who embark upon this journey may become frustrated. They may be lacking in preparation for the business and commercial issues they encounter; the hard financial realities and messy complexity and constraints of architectural practice. They may not have developed the communication skills to be able to persuade the clients, financiers, planners, building control officers, builders, lawyers, journalists, building users and citizenry that they encounter in the course of their work of the value of architecture, and the benefits that their ideas and designs will bring. They may feel overwhelmed by the sheer number of factors that conspire to influence the making of buildings and the associated challenges and obstacles that come with them. The emerging architect might also sense that perhaps clients, and moreover the wider public, do not fully connect with or understand the value of what architects do, and thus perhaps begin to feel an absence of the appreciation that all humans of necessity crave.

The high-profile achievements of the latest *starchitects* might also feed this need for positive feedback, and maybe even a sense of envy, certainly a desire for success. However, the fundamental driver for most architects is simply to do good work for the benefit of business and society, fairly rewarded, and for this to be recognised in a broad sense. Just as there is nothing wrong with ambition, neither is there with the search for recognition. Both are human impulses of the most natural kind.

This book therefore focuses on seeking to provide some practical insights into the more general skills that the architect needs, in addition to their design skills and specialist knowledge of building construction, in order to survive and prosper in a highly competitive and testing marketplace. It is an examination of the elements of psychology, sociology, marketing, communications, economics, persuasion and resource management that are relevant to success in architecture, but that do not necessarily explicitly feature in the education and training of the contemporary architect. Our concern will be to check that we are equipped with the softer, more intangible skills needed to reach our goals in this most demanding field.

As well as prompting some thoughts about the things we probably ought to know in order to succeed in architecture, on our route we will explore some diversions that might lead you to question how success in architecture might actually be measured, and suggest that there may in fact be more than one set of outcomes that represent the achievement of success. Ideally, I hope that if you read this book you will feel that you have a better insight into both the opportunities and the challenges of a career in the world of architecture, and a sense of how your own skills, talents and abilities might best contribute and what your own goals might be in the short, medium and long term.

WHAT THIS BOOK WON'T DO FOR YOU

Let's be honest. What this book won't do is guarantee you success.

HOW MIGHT THIS BOOK BE OF USE?

Some of the contents of this book may just seem like common sense, or even a statement of the obvious. Of course, this may be because they are in fact true and therefore not without value; you can't really argue with that, can you? Clearly, there may be some things with which you disagree or which you find provocative. I hope they will at least give pause for thought and prompt you to evaluate some of the less obvious aspects of the work of the architect that are nevertheless crucial to successful outcomes. Above all, I hope that it may help you in a small way towards achieving a career in architecture that is rewarding personally and professionally, and profitable!

This book comes in two parts:

Part 1 consists of 21 lessons that are important to success in architecture; these concepts aren't necessarily to be found on the curriculum in a school of architecture. In fact they never have been and perhaps never will.

Part 2 contains some wise words from 12 architects who have each found success on their own terms in the world of architecture.

Throughout the book, I've included some interesting facts and figures and some snappy quotes from the world of architecture, all to act as subliminal brain food to entertain you along the way.

Adrian Dobson
September 2014

"The student in architecture has also many and great difficulties to encounter, but they may be all overcome by reasonable assiduity, and proper application. He must be conversant in arithmetic, geometry, mechanics and hydraulics; and [be able] to explain his ideas with clearness, correctness and effect."

Sir John Soane[1]

01__David Watkin (Ed), *Sir John Soane: The Royal Academy Lectures* (Cambridge: Cambridge University Press, 2000), p.28. "Reproduced by permission of Cambridge University Press."

PART/1

21 THINGS YOU WON'T LEARN IN ARCHITECTURE SCHOOL

01_____In architecture, it's a long road to success

02_____There is more than one type of successful architect

03_____Architectural practices come in many forms

04_____Architecture doesn't exist in a vacuum

05_____You need to develop interests beyond architecture

06_____Architects think differently

07_____Speak in a language your audience understands

08_____Architects always work in teams

09_____Teams need leaders

10_____Architecture is a business

11_____Architects can learn business skills

12_____Architects have to sell and negotiate

13_____Work out what kind of architect you want to be and play to your strengths

14_____Communicate your unique message

15_____You need to understand fees

16_____Focus on people and process, not product

17_____Keep up to date with new technology and new thinking

18_____Look after your personal brand and networks

19_____Prizes matter – don't they?

20_____Construction sometimes involves conflict as well as collaboration

21_____There is no architecture without design

01 IN ARCHITECTURE, IT'S A LONG ROAD TO SUCCESS

Obviously, if your primary objective in life is to win fame, fortune and freedom through your vocation by the time you reach your 30th birthday, then architecture perhaps isn't the best option for you. Unlike premiership footballers, rock musicians and reality television show contestants, few architects can achieve a high profile in the early part of their careers. While there are exceptions to all rules, architecture is in general a slow burn occupation. It is not without reason that one of the most successful competitions in the UK aimed at supporting the development of emerging architectural design talent was given the title '40.under 40'.

It seems that architecture is more akin to the life of the long-distance runner than that of the 100m sprinter, doesn't it. Talent must obviously be important, but the dedication and time needed to establish the experience, reputation and credibility to sustain a successful position at the top of the architecture profession suggest that reserves of energy, resilience and stamina must surely also be of vital importance.

The internationally prestigious RIBA Gold Medal is awarded in recognition of a lifetime's work. Similarly, the most generously funded of all architectural awards, the Pritzker Prize, seems to take the view that an architect's merit is difficult to assess until a certain maturity has been reached. The Pritzker Prize honours 'living architects whose built work demonstrates a combination of those qualities of talent, vision, and commitment, which has produced consistent and significant contributions to humanity and the built environment through the art of architecture'.[1] Not exactly a pithy definition, but the sense of trepidation that honouring an architect who is still alive may in fact be unwisely premature is palpable.

The first 10 winners of the RIBA Gold Medal were:

Charles Robert Cockerell (1848, United Kingdom)

Luigi Canina (1849, Italy)

Sir Charles Barry (1850, United Kingdom)

Thomas Leverton Donaldson (1851, United Kingdom)

Leo von Klenze (1852, Germany)

Sir Robert Smirke (1853, United Kingdom)

Philip Hardwick (1854, United Kingdom)

Jacques Ignace Hittorff (1855, France)

Sir William Tite (1856, United Kingdom)

Owen Jones (1857, United Kingdom)

Friedrich August Stüler (1858, Germany)

Sir George Gilbert Scott (1859,United Kingdom)

01__http://www.pritzkerprize.com/about/purpose

//
Don't view it as a tragedy if
you lose out on a job; there
will be reasons. Re-focus on
the next opportunity, which
may be transformational //
Simon Allford

The winners between 2001 and 2014:

Jean Nouvel (2001, France)

Archigram (2002, United Kingdom)

Rafael Moneo (2003, Spain)

Rem Koolhaas (2004, Netherlands)

Frei Otto (2005, Germany)

Toyo Ito (2006, Japan)

Herzog and de Meuron (2007, Switzerland)

Edward Cullinan (2008, United Kingdom)

Álvaro Siza Vieira (2009, Portugal)

I M Pei (2010, China/USA)

David Chipperfield (2011, United Kingdom)

Herman Hertzberger (2012, The Netherlands)

Peter Zumthor (2013, Switzerland)

Joseph Rykwert (2014, Poland/United Kingdom)

What do these lists of names tell us about the characteristics of those architects deemed to have achieved the greatest success and held in the highest esteem?

The lack of a single woman is the most striking aspect,[2] and although this award now seems to have a broader international outlook it remains largely Euro-centric. Perhaps these biases reflect the unconscious predilections and intangible cultural assumptions of the RIBA Honours Committee, for they surely cannot really reflect a lack of achievement by women and the inhabitants of other continents. Nevertheless, important studies in both Australia and the United Kingdom have provided strong evidence that a lack of flexible working opportunities and relatively low levels of remuneration in comparison with other professions at mid-career stage act as a major barrier to women achieving senior positions in the architecture profession in greater numbers. This perhaps provides further evidence of the slow burn nature of the architect's career, in which staying competitive in the race throughout your thirties and forties seems to be vital for success.

02__Similarly, of the 38 winners of the Pritzker Prize only 2 laureates have been female: Zaha Hadid and Kazuyo Sejima.

There was a time (the past often seems to be a golden age) when a young, unknown, relatively inexperienced architect might establish a significant practice through winning an open architectural competition. However, we now live in more cautious times, when risk must always be managed, and such opportunities seem to be few and far between. Clients seem to prefer the reassurance of an established track record when appointing architects (even where competitions are used to select architects they are now increasingly likely to use a list of pre-selected invited firms rather than open entries); indeed, it seems increasingly difficult to achieve commissions for any particular building type, whether it be a school, a hospital or a housing development, without a portfolio of successfully completed projects within that sector. There is no shortage of older, experienced architects who are willing to provide their services. The majority of young, start-up practices have to cut their teeth in the bespoke housing sector or on the more imaginative fringes of mainstream practice.

However, younger architects bring their own skills and attributes: the ability to think beyond conventional modes of practices and services, a willingness to self-generate projects through activities such as community engagement and temporary architecture, and not least a knowledge of and affinity with new and emerging information and design technologies. Such assets are less likely to feature in the toolkit of their mid and later career peers.

The path between working as an employee for a practice and moving to starting a new practice, either alone or in partnership with others, is a well-worn one in architecture. It is much more commonplace in architecture than in other professional and business services disciplines, and is perhaps one of the reasons why there are relatively few truly large architectural businesses. Particularly in times of recession, when larger practices may be reducing staffing levels and opportunities for promotion are infrequent, there is a tendency for the profession to fragment through large numbers of new start-ups. The culture of the individual design visionary perpetuated by both the architectural education system and the architectural press is also a strong driver for many architects to establish their own practices.

Regarding when to make such a move, opinion seems to be divided. Some argue that establishing a practice at a young age brings dynamism, innovation and perhaps a healthy

// Without the breadth of experience I gained before setting up my own practice I would have been less well prepared for what I do now. You need experience to provide you with credibility with clients //
Marianne Davys

//
You have to maintain a constant
course, and not allow yourself
to be knocked off your route
by recession or politics. You
need a plan that will work in the
short term but that will also
last you for decades //
Bill Dunster

disregard for some of the risks and barriers to success that older and wiser heads, with mortgages to pay and perhaps mouths to feed, would find inhibiting. The youthful characteristics that are so successfully fuelling the start-up culture in the web tech sector can be applied in architecture. Others suggest that the practice of architecture, with its myriad artistic, professional, technical, administrative and legal aspects, is one in which experience counts for a great deal. It is certainly the case that age and experience can often bring a credibility that provides reassurance to clients. The opportunities for developing a successful and rewarding architectural career at a senior level within an established architectural practice should also not be discounted. An existing business will have the infrastructure in terms of business systems, information technology, human resources and marketing that has to be developed from scratch when starting a new practice, and it may offer career progressions to interesting positions that are more focused and can perhaps be more closely matched to an individual architect's strengths and aspirations.

Whatever flight path is adopted, it certainly seems prudent for the emerging professional architect to try to gain early experience of the whole design and delivery processes – briefing and concept design, the planning process, technical design, works on site, post-occupancy services. Working in a range of different sizes and types of practice and sectors of activity also brings clear benefits and helps in understanding the range of roles and activities that are encompassed by the (protected) title of architect, and working out how and where your talents can best be applied.

So, in contemplating a career path in a profession that tends to be dominated by the more mature practitioner, it is important to remember that new minds have much to bring to the party; to ensure that you work out what your unique assets are and do not undervalue them; and not to be pushed off course by the inevitable bumps and barriers in the road. Staying in the game is half the battle!

02

THERE IS MORE THAN ONE TYPE OF SUCCESSFUL ARCHITECT

The notion that the figure known as the *starchitect* emerged as a fully developed new life form sometime in the early 1990s is a fallacy. When I was an architecture student in Manchester in the 1980s, genteelly ageing professors still spoke in reverential terms about the 'big 3': Mies van der Rohe, Le Corbusier and Frank Lloyd Wright. The influence of these three architect practitioner/philosophers was still surprisingly strong at that time, along with that of the more taciturn and ambiguous Alva Aalto. So we might conclude that the concept of the architect as celebrity, albeit within the somewhat rarefied circle of the 'high' arts, is far from a new phenomenon; indeed its roots certainly go back as far as the 17th and 18th centuries.

A blockbuster exhibition at the Royal Academy in London in 1986 effectively cast James Stirling, Norman Foster and Richard Rogers as the new 'big 3', in the UK context at least. The fact that Foster and Rogers have gone from strength to strength in developing truly global practices suggests that this was a successful strategy. This informal star system certainly became a worldwide phenomenon during the 1990s and 2000s, with figures such as Frank Gehry and Rem Koolhaas gaining international profiles comparable with those of high-profile fine artists, if not perhaps hitting the heights of fame that can be achieved in the fields of business, sport and popular entertainment.

At the conference organised by the International Union of Architects (UIA) in Istanbul in 2000, the Iraqi-born UK-based architect Zaha Hadid was welcomed into a hall containing more than 5,000 enthusiastic delegates with a roar of excitement and near hysteria of the kind that would normally be associated with a stadium concert by the latest boy or girl pop band. Her appearance perhaps had a particular cultural significance for an audience of younger architects and students in Istanbul at a specific moment in time. Nevertheless, the reception could have been no more electric if Elvis had emerged alive and well into the lights on the stage (although of course most of the audience might not have recognised him).

As the first real female architectural superstar, and one with a highly recognisable, exciting and unique approach to the development of architectural forms, combined with a distinctive personal philosophy, image and charisma, Zaha Hadid has a particular significance for architects, and the ability to exert a cultural influence beyond the narrower confines of the profession. Architects and architectural journalists and the wider media now frequently refer to 'Zaha', using the single-name idiom usually reserved in mainstream journalism for international pop idols like Bono, Madonna and Beyoncé. Zaha therefore can be seen to represent the first true embodiment of the architect as both personality and brand, a trail blazed by the likes of Richard Branson and Victoria Beckham in mainstream commercial culture.

A small, select group of architects now has the type of creative credibility aligned with media profile that actually enables them to act as a magnetic force in attracting publicity and funding to projects, so that they can add value even before they put pen to paper.

The cult of the *starchitect* is of course of benefit to the wider architecture profession, but also potentially problematic. Anything less than the achievement of this individual status might now be interpreted as a failed career, but this surely cannot be the case, can it? For a start, if you scratch the surface of each of these super-brands, there is usually at least one canny collaborator, and often a tight senior team, dealing with some of the commercial and practical pragmatics necessary to run an architectural practice as a global operation. Indeed, historically many of the most successful architectural practices were a marriage of two, or more, distinctive characters, one perhaps possessed of a clear and strong theoretical and design vision and the other more grounded in business and project delivery.

The advertising industry is informative in this regard with its clear separation of functions between account management and creative directors – something that is rarely explicitly recognised within the operational structures of architects' practices, despite the many obvious parallels between the two industries.

However, there have been a number of attempts to reflect the functional separation of conceptual design and detailed design for construction within an architectural practice structure. In more recent years we have seen some approaches to procurement in which different practices have been employed on the same project to carry out these two elements of initial design development and technical design delivery.

The post-Second World War adoption across architectural education of a Bauhaus-inspired teaching methodology, itself derived at least partially from the earlier French Beaux-Arts tradition, which has gradually developed into the unit teaching system now employed almost universally in one form or another in schools of architecture across the globe, has given primacy to the development of the architect as an original thinker and designer, concerned

// I don't think there is any substitute for working out for yourself what it is you are trying to do, not following someone else's approach. Do you want to be a follower or to set the rules? //
Bill Dunster

//
Career development routes in
architecture are very ill-defined.
Do you go it alone and set
up a practice, or commit to
an existing practice and try
to move up the hierarchy? //
Caroline Buckingham

predominantly with the process of design and production. This has perhaps been at the expense of the development of a wider range of social, business and communication skills, and arguably a deeper knowledge of architectural history, that characterised earlier forms of architectural education and training, such as the British system of pupillage, in which an apprentice architect was largely trained on the job through a form of indenture.

This transformation has served the profession well, producing several generations of highly creative and innovative architects, and enabling the alumni of the most high-profile schools to influence arguably not just architectural culture, but also more general design culture. It has provided architects with a specific skill set and approach to problem-solving that they can offer as a unique selling point. At the same time, it has left architects less well equipped to maintain their traditional role of project leadership, as other professionals and design and build procurement methods have competed hard in this territory.

It is to state the obvious, but true, to say that for many clients the capability to design to a high standard is taken as a given within the architect's toolkit. Regardless of your own assessment of your design abilities, it will normally be assumed that your competency as a building designer is assured by the professional letters – such as AIA, HKIA or RIBA – with which architects adorn their business cards, letterheads and websites, and in many projects other aspects are likely to be equally important in deciding the selection of the architect. A track record of successful project delivery, deep knowledge of a particular client sector or specialist building type, the development of a particular culture or approach to working with clients and stakeholders, or networking skills can be the keys to opening the doors to work streams. So it is clear that a reputation can be established on aspects other than just design skills alone, but establishing credibility, and a profile and clear identity, is nevertheless essential.

Do you want to create a reputation for excellent client service, delivering projects of high quality on time and to budget? Do you want to design award-winning buildings that are published in the most prestigious architectural journals and admired by your peers? Do you want to create works of artistic integrity? Do you want to achieve commercial success and own a Ferrari? Do you want to create a practice that reflects your social and political values? Do you want to create stable and rewarding employment in a stimulating working environment? All of this?

//
The more architects who enter into different types of private and public sector organisations, the better it will be for our society //

Shankari Raj Edgar

Perhaps the first step to a successful career in architecture is to work out the metrics against which you are going to evaluate your achievements.

In fact many architects migrate to roles in architecture, construction and other related industries that are far beyond the confines of what might be defined as mainstream practice. There are many architects who develop highly successful careers in areas as diverse as development management, city planning, central and local government, estate management and product design. Many large contracting and project management organisations are headed by architects; this is not the exclusive preserve of surveyors and engineers. Architects can make excellent clients and developers. The design and construction sector is all the richer for this. Architects may also head off in other directions, towards academia, research or journalism, for example. It is thought that at any one time up to a third of the UK architects on the register maintained by the Architects Registration Board (ARB) are not currently involved in activity that might recognisably conform to a traditional model of architectural practice. We need not be trapped in traditional roles.

Perhaps the most critical factor is to appraise realistically and honestly in which type of practice or role you can best and most effectively operate. What type of architect are you best equipped to be? What would success look like for you?

03

ARCHITECTURAL PRACTICES COME IN MANY FORMS

The report *The Future for Architects?*, produced in 2011 by the RIBA's Building Futures think tank,[3] identified a number of distinct types of architects' practice that each faced their own challenges and opportunities, including:

Small local general practice

International star architect

Specialist niche practice

Traditional regional delivery-driven practice

Global interdisciplinary consultancy

Build-own-operate-transfer designer

Design houses/creative agency

Medium-sized design-led practice

Small metropolitan boutique practice

Clearly, the architecture profession is not one homogenous set of look-alike businesses, but rather a whole series of multiple, parallel professional models of operation. There is a world of differences between the large metropolitan office of a global practice, a medium-sized design studio in a regional city, a specialist practice focused on particular technologies or sectors, and a very small rural practice working in a clearly defined contextual setting, in terms of working cultures and business models, risks and rewards, and day-to-day activity. A practice of 20 working in a single studio space will inevitably have an internal dynamic different from that of a practice of 50 people.

In Part 2 of this book we will be hearing from a dozen architects who have all found success and reward in the profession across a large range of different practice sizes, types and cultures. This clearly demonstrates that it is possible to construct a career in many different types of practice setting. The challenge is to work out which type of environment will best enable you to thrive and prosper. Smaller practices offer the possibility of earlier exposure to the full range of architectural activity, from strategic definition and briefing to in-use services, as set out in the RIBA Plan of Work.[4] A larger practice may offer a wider number of niche roles and may enable you to deploy your specific talents in a more focused way.

In reality there are a series of different architectural professions encompassing those models set out in the Building Futures report and many others as well. One key emerging trend in

---

03__Building Futures, *The Future for Architects? Who will design our buildings in 2025?*, www.buildingfutures.org.uk 2011.

04__www.ribaplanofwork.com

//
In the end, there are only a
limited number of opportunities
to create the one-off, iconic
works of architecture, and we
need to make sure that the
general quality of the buildings
we produce is high //

John Assael

the UK is a growing difference in market focus and business model between larger practices of over, say, 200 staff (still small in the context of other professional services sectors), which increasingly operate in a global market, often with multiple offices located in key hubs spread across different time zones and which recruit from a worldwide talent pool, and the rest of the profession, which tends to focus on more proximate markets. One key choice that faces the emerging professional architect is which of these two fundamentally different models has the greater appeal to their instincts and ambitions.

It is good to remember that the protean nature of the architecture profession gives plenty of options for personal growth and career development, and you need not feel constrained by a single model of what practice might be. We are spoilt for choice.

04 ARCHITECTURE DOESN'T EXIST IN A VACUUM

In its 2006 publication *The Value Handbook: getting the most from your buildings and spaces*,[5] the UK Commission for Architecture and the Built Environment (CABE) identified six different types of value created by the built environment:

Exchange value (the commercial value of a building as a commodity to be traded)

Use value (the contribution of a building to organisational outcomes)

Image value (the value of a building in terms of corporate identity, brand, prestige, vision or reputation)

Social value (the contribution that developments make to social interaction, identity and inclusion, and to civic pride)

Environmental value (the value added arising from a concern for intergenerational equity, the protection of biodiversity and the precautionary principle in relation to consumption of finite resources, including the immediate benefits to local health and pollution)

Cultural value (the less tangible benefits in terms of contribution to such matters as townscape, context and sense of place)

In one sense this list was obviously created to set out an argument for the overall value of architecture, but it is interesting to reflect that it is in itself a very useful analysis of the ways in which the practice of architecture does not, and cannot, exist in a vacuum. Above all architecture is a practical art, at least in application, and must engage with the society in which it exists. Social, cultural and economic factors are always at play, and the emerging architect is unlikely to see projects realised without understanding the broader and specific contexts within which projects are placed.

The above list would suggest that, just for starters, at the very minimum an understanding of the following six subjects needs to be added to the extra-curricular studies of every architecture student:

Development economics

Organisational and workplace studies

Public relations and marketing

Sociology and politics

Environmental science

Liberal arts

05__CABE, *The Value Handbook: getting the most from your buildings and spaces*, http://webarchive.nationalarchives. gov.uk/20110118095356/http://www.cabe.org.uk/files/the-value-handbook.pdf 2006.

It would probably be a matter of surprise to the general public, although not to experienced clients, to be told that most architects emerge from an extensive professional education with only the slightest of insights into development economics. And yet many architects are engaged in day-to-day activity where such aspects are a key driver of decision-making and where they have to negotiate and collaborate with funders and developers.

The undoubted message is that the successful architect needs a curiosity about the world that reaches beyond the sometimes closed sanctum of architectural discourse and design methodology.

Jeremy Till is Head of Central St Martins College and Pro Vice-chancellor of the University of the Arts London, and a partner at Sarah Wrigglesworth Architects. In his book *Architecture Depends*, he examines the contingent nature of architecture and its dependency on the messy complexity of people, politics, economics and numerous other external factors and agents:

> Of course all human actions in any given field are dependent on others to a greater or lesser extent: no one is fully isolated from outside forces. However, architecture is peculiarly exposed to these external dependencies. An accountant, say, may place the fluid finances of a company into the order of a standardised system of measurement. The artist may block the world out during moments of creative conception. The lawyer has recourse to a documented and reasonably stable body of case law ... An architect has neither the luxury of solitude, nor the precision of standard methods, nor ... the comfort of a stable epistemology. Architecture is dependent on others at every stage of its journey from initial sketch to inhabitation.[6]

Of the six values identified by CABE, most successful architects will probably have certain aspects, related to their principal sectors of work, in which they are most expert and able to provide and demonstrate the value of their contribution, but knowledge of and the ability to engage in informed dialogue across the full range of these facets is a clear advantage to those committed to establishing an architectural career.

If there is a common perception among the profession that its practitioners are no longer held in as high regard by society as they once were, reflected in a perceived reduced standing within the construction industry and lower levels of remuneration, then some of the blame for this may lie in an unwillingness to provide more general leadership and contribution to the life of communities and nations. This raises the issue of the role of the architect in society.

For many years Sir Sydney Chapman was the only architect member of the House of Commons, the lower house of the UK Parliament. Sir Sydney was a reliable and eloquent spokesman on matters relating to architecture and the role of the architect in society, but in parliament he was a lone voice among the serried ranks of lawyers, bankers, consultants and policy wonks. Lord Rogers has been the other nationally prominent representative of the input of the architecture profession on the national stage in the UK, with a seat in the upper chamber of the UK Parliament, and he has been a consistent campaigner on matters relating to the design and development of our cities, in particular London. However, the voice and contribution of the architect is not commonly heard at a national political level. An exception to this rule of

---

06__Jeremy Till, *Architecture Depends* (Cambridge, MA: MIT Press, 2009), p.45. Reproduced by permission of the MIT Press.

//
As an architect you are living
in the world of ideas. You need
to understand the people;
the places; the city //
Simon Allford

thumb is Brazil, where architects such as Oscar Niemeyer, Lina Bo Bardi and Jaime Lerner have created a tradition of serious political engagement. Generally, though, in recent decades, the profession has focused its political activity on influencing the legislative and regulatory context for practice and construction, rather than contributing to the big social, cultural and economic discourse of politics.

The election of George Ferguson, a highly successful architect and entrepreneur and former President of the RIBA, to the post of Mayor of Bristol is an exciting development. Bristol will be a fascinating test bed for what the particular skill set of an architect can bring to civic leadership in the 21st century. Clearly there is a role for architects to contribute both personal insights and professional impact, particularly at a city level.

A greater willingness on the part of architects at local and national levels to get stuck in to political and cultural debate would signify a return to a period of deeper engagement with society and also perhaps promote a return of civic pride. It could be of nothing but benefit to the perception and profile of the profession, and would perhaps equip architects to speak 'human' a little more often.

05 YOU NEED TO DEVELOP INTERESTS BEYOND ARCHITECTURE

The two most significant characteristics that mark humans out from the rest of the animal kingdom, and have enabled our extraordinary dominance and extravagant exploitation of our lonely planet, are the ability to rapidly adapt to change and the capacity to specialise. The division of early societies into farming, craft and warrior classes was the start of a unique journey that culminated in the complex division of labour of the industrial revolution.

In this sense, architects as a professional group represent a highly specialised unit of production within complex industrial and post-industrial societies.

Of course, the practice of architecture requires both an in-depth understanding of the process of designing and making buildings and also a broad knowledge of the vast array of economic, sociological and environmental factors that influence the context in which the practice of architecture takes place. Nevertheless, architecture is a specialised field of endeavour; indeed, the establishment of professional associations, registration boards and learned bodies represents a public declaration of this specialisation. All specialist fields can become self-referential, and architecture and architects are not immune to this affliction. This can make it difficult for architects to put across their messages within a broader sociological context; arguably, it often creates a barrier between architects and their ultimate clients – the users of their buildings – and frequently leaves architects ill-equipped to communicate effectively even with their colleagues in the rest of the construction industry.

In order to be able to connect and interact it is important to engage with ideas from beyond the sometimes vacuum-packed world of architecture and architects. If your work takes place in specific sectors, say education, health or housing, then an understanding of the policy, economic and regulatory factors that impact on those sectors is crucial if you are to be able to speak the language of your clients and stakeholders and relate to the culture of those particular sectors. Jeremy Till urges architects to avoid retreating to the comfortable confines of architectural abstraction:

> Best then, as an architect, to get out there, to stare one's own fragility in the face. To be human. Remember who you were before you were branded an architect. Remember that you too inhabit this world. Remember that you too use buildings, occupy space. And remember that users, you included, are more than abstractions or ideals; they are imperfect, multiple, political, and all the better for it.[7]

07__Jeremy Till, *Architecture Depends* (Cambridge, MA: MIT Press, 2009), p.126. Reproduced by permission of The MIT Press.

//

Architecture is always enmeshed in the big societal issues; subject to them and an essential part of the solution //

Sunand Prasad

A broad exposure to a range of cultural, technological and intellectual fields is therefore highly desirable. As we have seen, architecture does not exist in a vacuum and many ideas that influence the profession in both creative and business terms come from other fields of endeavour.

//

I am interested in the connection between different aspects of society, culture, technology. This is really what architecture is all about – joining up a diversity of human activities and trying to create an equitable future //

Bill Dunster

06 ARCHITECTS THINK DIFFERENTLY

For a moment, let's take a stereotyped view of the typical architect. We all know that architects are well paid, wear black (or sometimes more daringly red), and if possible ignore their clients so that they can design what they want. Architects regularly feature in the top five in popular surveys of the profession whose members would make the most desirable marriage partners. Interestingly, they rarely feature highly in surveys of those most satisfied with their work, in which hairdressers and gardeners regularly emerge on top of the pile. The desirability of architects as marriage partners suggests that the perception of a prosperous and stylish professional still persists, despite what architects may think or know to the contrary, or perhaps it is inspired by other more altruistic characteristics of a profession concerned to create a better world for its inhabitants. The cliché about never letting the client's wishes stand in the way of the best solution certainly retains enough currency to support the assumption that it encapsulates at least a grain of truth.

There is one area of stereotyping of architects that I believe clearly does relate to a widely shared characteristic among architects. That is the way in which architects think. Evidence abounds to suggest that architects are in the main right-brain thinkers, with associated factors such as left-handedness and dyslexia more common among architects than among the general population. Certainly, the architectural education system encourages this tendency even where it does not necessarily sit as a predisposition within the student. The predominant Bauhaus-inspired studio teaching ethos encourages the student to abandon preconceptions about design and creativity developed in mainstream primary and secondary education and to begin again with a blank slate.

This different way of thinking brings both advantages and disadvantages. In general, architects work via a process of synthesis rather than analysis; architects default to the representation of ideas and processes through drawings and diagrams rather than words or numerical expression; architects project visions rather than narratives. This can mean that the architect brings a unique approach to problem-solving and project development, which the other professions involved in the commissioning, design and construction of buildings cannot offer. Some people call this creative, problem-solving approach 'design thinking'.

Design thinking can be characterised as being an empirical, solution-finding approach as opposed to a problem-solving, analytical approach. In itself it can be applied in a range of business contexts, often with innovative and creative results that can bring great entrepreneurial benefits. Indeed, design thinking is increasingly being applied to the design of services and processes far outside the traditional design fields of architecture, landscape, fashion, graphics and products, but it is not the dominant thinking approach within broader business and society. Consequently, architects can face communication barriers when dealing with the left-brain

//

I think that one very important
attribute is having empathy
for the people you are working
for and with ... You need to
be able to tune in to other
people's frequencies as
quickly as possible //
Satwinder Samra

thinkers that make up the majority of the population of financiers, developers, accountants, lawyers, surveyors, engineers, journalists and building users with which they must effectively engage if they are to be successful. This is simply because the ways of describing and resolving problems are not commonly shared and are rarely mutually valued. The scope for miscommunication and misunderstanding is significant. Throughout the educational process; architecture students spend most of their time selling and communicating their design ideas and design thinking to architects, rarely to clients or co-professionals, further increasing the potential for cultural isolation. At the same time, this different way of thinking is both inevitable and the core differentiator of what the architect uniquely has to offer. If architecture is a blend of the art and science of building, then ultimately when the chips are down it is the artistic that must predominate.

So architects need to be aware of this different approach and exploit this special element of their skill set at every appropriate opportunity, but at the same time they need to be

//

I think that architects always
seek a solution that focuses
on the highest common
factor rather than the lowest
common denominator //
David Partridge

conscious of the need to turn off their architect brain when circumstances require a more mainstream, rationalist approach if they are to avoid alienating or confusing their collaborators and clients.

It is important to remember that architects do think differently, and this exceptional strength mustn't be allowed to turn into a weakness.

07 SPEAK IN A LANGUAGE YOUR AUDIENCE UNDERSTANDS

Any standard business textbook will tell you that high-level creative and technical skills and specialist knowledge are essential to achieve progress in the early stages of a professional career, but it is the less tangible soft skills around communication and human relations that are key to unlocking access to join the higher levels of leadership in firms and organisations. I believe that these skills sometimes present a particular challenge to architects, and therefore learning about communication should be a high priority for the architect who wishes to succeed. This principle applies to communication in all its forms: visual, verbal and in writing. Although architecture is a visual art, the importance of the role of the spoken and written word should not be underestimated, and as in design, less is often more; it is important not to complicate the message unnecessarily.

In his book *Museum Without Walls*, Jonathan Meades, the iconoclastic British author and broadcaster, points an astute finger at the worrying tendency of architects to obfuscate their messages in a secret language, which is entirely mysterious and mystifying to those outside the profession:

> This most public of endeavours, is practised by people who inhabit a smugly hermetic milieu which is cultish. If this sounds far-fetched just consider the way that initiates of this cult describe outsiders as the *lay* public, *lay* writers and so on: it's the language of the priesthood. And like all cults its primary interest is its own interests, that is to say its survival, and in the triumph of its values – which means building. Architects, architectural critics, architectural theorists, the architectural press (which is little more than a deferential PR machine operated by sycophants whose tongue can injure a duodenum) – the entire quasi-cult is cosily conjoined by mutual dependence and by an ingrown, verruca-like jargon which derives from the more dubious end of American academe.[8]

Meades focuses his ire particularly on the coded language used by architects, but the point he makes is revealing of a general distance and lack of engagement that the profession often unwittingly, but sometimes intentionally, places between itself and the 'public'. This level of disconnect between the profession and the society it serves seems to be at best dubious if not damaging. Reinforcing this division through the use of *archispeak* hardly seems the most effective way to communicate design ideas and to persuade people of the validity and value of those ideas.

08__Jonathan Meades, *Museum Without Walls* (London: Unbound, 2012), p.10. Reproduced by permission of Unbound.

//

The client wants your expertise, which is the most precious thing you have to offer; but unless you can communicate your expertise it remains locked up //
Sunand Prasad

Based on my own experiences of meeting and listening to many architects during the course of professional life, I would assert that the architects of the highest design calibre and business acumen who achieve success are generally also very effective communicators. They combine their design skills with an ability and willingness to engage with clients, stakeholders and the wider society of communities and politics. Successful architects have a desire to explain their ideas and working methods to a range of audiences and the ability to put across a narrative explaining their work in accessible terms. The capability to do this enthusiastically and persuasively, without resorting to jargon, can be a powerful tool for the architect who wishes to engage with the community of people that influence and shape our built environment, encompassing the world of architecture and architects but also looking outwards and beyond the inward-looking confines of architectural discourse.

Developing and refining a message so that it can be taken out to a wider audience offers opportunities to establish a reputation as a leader in your field. By contrast, pitching up as a member of a mystical professional elite creates the risk of isolation in a socio-cultural

//

You can be an outstanding designer, but you also have to be able to get your message across. It is important to be able to talk with passion about your design without coming over as arrogant //
Caroline Buckingham

bubble, with little opportunity to influence the decision-making that sets the context in which architecture is practised.

For over a decade the RIBA has organised an annual small practice conference: Guerrilla Tactics. A much loved feature of this event is the closing Live Pitch session, in which emerging and highly talented small firms compete to pitch their ideas for a design commission to a panel of professional clients. The most striking and unchanging feature of these sessions is that it is never really the design ideas presented that finally determine the winning outcome – the design work is always universally of high quality – but rather the ability of the competing practices to explain the story of their proposals with a tight and timely narrative that touches a chord with their audience of clients; it is in the end a form of performance.

08 ARCHITECTS ALWAYS WORK IN TEAMS

The cult of the *starchitect* might lead you to conclude that successful architects are strongly independent visionaries, able to operate without the safety net of support teams or trusted advisers. But of course, as we have already seen, these branded superstars are invariably backed, and must also effectively manage, sophisticated teams of partners, directors and staff. (The same applies, of course, in the world of fine art; think of Andy Warhol and the Factory, or Amish Kapoor, or Jeff Koons.) The most successful architects are often leaders, but they are also team workers.

Collaboration is at the heart of the process of designing, procuring and constructing buildings. Whether it is engaging with client and stakeholder teams to understand the strategic aims and objectives of a project, drawing upon the strengths and individual expertise of colleagues within the architect's own studio, sharing ideas and information with the engineers, cost consultants and other specialists within the design team, or working with builders and specialist sub-contractors and suppliers to solve the very practical problems and logistics of construction, architects are constantly in the midst of cooperative processes with a high level of mutual dependency.

Architects work in teams in their own practices, with other consultants in the design team, with client teams, with contractors and specialist sub-contractors … and the list goes on. A strength of architectural education is its use of a project-based teaching model as an analogue for the real-world activity of architectural design, but the element of team-working and collaboration, and in particular its interdisciplinary aspects, is difficult, if not impossible, to simulate in the educational environment, so it is rarely attempted with vigour and conviction. The nascent architect emerges from the school of architecture blinking into the harsh light of the real world of practice in which individual drive, creativity, knowledge and talent, though valuable assets, are simply a starting point for developing a career. Often the real world of practice is perhaps not quite what was imagined. Architecture school was hard and life is not going to get any easier. Learning how to work effectively with others is essential to survival. What lies ahead is the demanding hard work of collaborating with colleagues, co-consultants, client teams, contractors and sub-contractors, many of whom bring quite different professional values, terminology and methods of working to the game.

The skill set needed to facilitate this effective collaboration and coordination of a complex project delivery team is becoming ever more demanding. Where once the architect was the natural leader of the design and construction process whose credentials were unchallenged, recent decades have seen innovations in procurement and the establishment of new professional management roles that have to various degrees undermined this hegemony. The highly respected Dutch architect Herman Hertzberger, interviewed by David Rodgers in

//
It is important to work with
the very best people you
can. You need the right mix
of complementary skills
in your team //
Sunand Prasad

Building Design magazine following his announcement as the winner of the 2012 RIBA Royal Gold Medal, lamented the diminishing role of the architect:

> We are not recognised as important as we once were many years ago … We're not buried next to the king anymore. Architects have to be happy to get a job and say yes to everything. The role has been diminished and we're just one of the people making a building. We're not the master of the whole thing anymore.[9]

This means that the contemporary architect often needs to exercise leadership without the benefit of automatic authority, and must therefore be able to draw upon a broader range of team-working skills.

In reality, most building projects require the architect to demonstrate vision and exercise leadership regardless of the formal roles and contractual relationships within the project team, but this must be done in the context of an often complex and diverse collaborative structure. When a major decision needs to be made or an intricate problem needs to be resolved, it is most frequently the architect that the other members of the design and construction team and the client turn to. This central role as the only player with a comprehensive overview of the project as an integrated whole is a tremendous asset and source of power for the architect. However, without the ability to take ownership of the project and persuade, cajole and incentivise the rest of the team to buy into the common purpose, the architect is unlikely to be successful.

All this takes place in the context of a construction industry where there are myriad potential procurement arrangements, a multitude of ways of assembling the project team and a plethora of contractual relationships. The architect might occasionally be employed directly by the end user(s) of a building but is just as likely to be reporting to a funder, developer, project manager or contractor. In fact, in the UK contractors acting as the architect's prime client now account for one fifth of total architects' fees.[10] The architect may be responsible for coordinating and integrating the work of a complex team of engineers, specialist designers

---

09__As quoted in 'Hertzberger laments fading role of architect', interview by David Rodgers in *Building Design*, 8 December 2011, http://www.bdonline.co.uk/hertzberger-laments-fading-role-of-architect/5029022.article

10__Source: RIBA Business Benchmarking Survey 2012/13.

//
We are very persuaded by
people who can demonstrate
excellence in sport or music,
because this shows an ability
to work in a team //
John Assael

and other consultants, some of whom they may be employing directly as sub-consultants while with others they may have no formal contractual relationship.

So while the architect may no longer still be king, leadership, both creative and managerial, must be provided, and this involves orchestrating an often complex team of players and managing multiple business relationships. Projects need champions and leadership that can promote a common vision and inspire a sense of common purpose, but the days of command and control are long gone. The central casting version of the architect as an individual hero is far from reality.

09 TEAMS NEED LEADERS

If you take a glance at the business titles in the non-fiction section of any bookseller or the titles of the articles in current business magazines, the word *leadership* is everywhere. Leadership is the new management. Managers are no longer implored just to demonstrate good organisational skills but also to provide the leadership that motivates and brings meaning to the work of their teams. The traditional image of the leader is that of the charismatic visionary, able to act as a catalyst for mobilisation of resources and the delivery of great change through force of personality and authenticity of belief; think Gandhi and Martin Luther King Jr, Margaret Thatcher and Winston Churchill, and perhaps Richard Branson and Steve Jobs in a business context. Nowadays a more subtle model of leadership is emerging to suit the culture and ethos of the times. It is recognised that leadership today also needs to come from within teams and organisations; that it cannot simply be imposed from above in a hierarchical fashion. In a sense, everyone needs to be a leader or exhibit leadership skills to at least some degree. From this comes the concept of leading up; the notion that as organisations become increasingly de-centralised and rely more upon networks of partners to achieve innovation, something that is already a well-established pattern of working in the construction sector, team members will need to exercise greater influence over their managers for mutual benefit. People at all levels within firms and multi-disciplinary teams can influence and persuade and bring useful ideas to the table. Of course, for this two-way communication and support to be effective requires the right mindset at all organisational levels and the willingness of partners, directors and managers to listen as well as direct.

The RIBA Plan of Work identifies several key leadership roles in the project team:[11]

Client – The party commissioning the design and construction of a project. The client may be an individual or a company or organisation.

Project Lead – Responsible for managing all aspects of the project and ensuring that the project is delivered in accordance with the Project Programme.

Lead Designer – Responsible for managing all aspects of the design, including the coordination of the design and the integration of specialist sub-contractors' design.

Construction Lead – Responsible for constructing the project and for providing construction advice in the early stages.

11__www.ribaplanofwork.com

Clearly there are a number of players within the industry who might feel able to take on the Project Lead role, but it would be to the benefit of both the architecture profession and the wider construction industry if more architects were willing to put themselves forward for project leadership.

It is of the greatest importance that architects lean in and take on the lead designer role. The last 30 years have seen a general tendency for architects to increasingly shy away from aspects of the management and coordination of the design process, and to relinquish elements of this to a range of other professional consultants and design managers. And yet the architect, with a high level of emotional and professional commitment to the quality of project outcome and a unique overview of the total design, is ideally placed to undertake this role. Indeed, I would argue that it is almost a dereliction of duty not to do so. Who else is really able to coordinate and integrate the increasingly complex design inputs from multiple sources (designers, contractors, sub-contractors, suppliers) into a meaningful design model?

Leadership involves the effective mobilisation of financial, intellectual, material and human resources, but it is the people element that is probably the most important and the most challenging. In the same way that the development of a great sports team or a great orchestra requires the bringing together of a group of players with different and complementary talents, so project teams and design teams need a range of different skills, and with this inevitably comes a diversity of personalities. Making the chemistry work effectively is more alchemy than science. The somewhat insular nature of architectural education does not necessarily prepare architects for the challenge of dealing with the myriad thinking styles and cultures that make up the typical project team, but it is an essential skill for effective leadership.

Demographic and cultural changes mean that the future leaders of the architecture profession will be managing much more diverse teams. By 2031, ethnic populations will make up 15% of the population in England and 37% in London. In 2014, women represented 47% of the total UK workforce, but only made up 22% of UK registrants with the Architects Registration Board (ARB) and 18% of the RIBA's UK chartered membership. Women are significantly under-represented at senior leadership levels within the profession, with information from the RIBA's Business Benchmarking Survey 2012/13 showing, that while women make up 40% of Part 1 architectural assistants, only 12% of equity partners and directors are female.[12] Various research studies have identified barriers that impact upon the progress of women and ethnic minorities in the profession and the factors related to socio-economic background that influence the make-up of the profession. As equality, diversity and inclusion become embedded as core ethical values in society and the changing demographics of an ageing population impact on the profile of the working population, it should be expected that the UK architecture profession will become more diverse and more reflective of the society it serves. This diversity will also be reflected in the leadership profile of the profession.

Diversity will also be manifested in the generational composition of teams. The *baby boomer* generation (born between approximately 1945 and 1965) is gradually approaching retirement, but the impact of the financial crisis on factors such as pension annuity rates means that many will continue to be active in the workforce, whether by choice or from financial necessity. As the demographically smaller *generation x* (born broadly between 1965 and 1980) increasingly enters managerial positions, the bulk of the workforce will be comprised of *generation y*

12__Source: RIBA Business Benchmarking Survey 2012/13.

//
You need leaders, but this industry
is all about collaboration and
so the ego needs to be both
expressed and supressed at
different times //
Simon Allford

(born 1980 to 2000), but hot on their heels are following the so-called digital natives of the *alpha generation* (the 'millennials'). For the first time, the workforce will contain four very different generational groups, sometimes dubbed the 4G workforce, each of which has its own motivational and leadership styles.

The *baby boomers* are generally considered to exhibit a high work ethic, and to be driven by status and salary, loyal to organisations and good at bringing fresh perspectives to problems. They are felt to be strong team players and generally dislike and seek to avoid direct conflict. They are likely to be challenged in managing the outwardly confident, sociable and technologically savvy *generation y*, whose members have high expectations of rapid advancement but nevertheless seek frequent feedback and reassurance when problems arise. *Generation y* employees are likely to be happy to switch employers frequently and may even run parallel careers, seeking work that is meaningful to them, and in the context of the architecture profession are unlikely to feel constrained by traditional concepts of architectural practice or what it means to be an architect. Squeezed between these two groups are the self-reliant *generation x*, with a preference for individual action rather than group working. They are reasonably happy in the world of online data, but nevertheless struggle with the always-on culture and lack of face-to-face engagement of their *generation y* colleagues. Seeking security, members of *generation x* remain reasonably loyal to firms but place a high value on flexible working arrangements and personal development opportunities. All will soon be learning to deal with the members of the emerging *alpha generation*, with their apparent lack of concern for personal privacy, total comfort with online collaboration, high emphasis on ethical issues such as tolerance, sustainability and social justice, and global outlook.

Coming to grips with the changing nature of leadership, the need to demonstrate leadership at all levels within teams and organisations, and the specific challenges of leadership in a more complex, fluid and diverse workforce are key issues facing professionals in all sectors. Giving some thought to how this all might play out in the context of the business of architecture will bring rewards for the emerging professional architect. The creation of architecture as realised built works is a highly collaborative process, with a high degree of dependency on the actions of complex delivery teams and external constraints. Some of what the individual architect needs to achieve successful outcomes is in their own hands, but much else depends on motivating and persuading others; in other words, offering leadership.

10 ARCHITECTURE IS A BUSINESS

Part of the appeal of architecture as a vocation is that it requires a combination of art, science and letters; if you like, it's the archetypal Renaissance profession. The conceptual model of what we now call an architect has its origins in the great cross-disciplinary figures of the Italian Renaissance. This model subsequently went through a further transformation in northern Europe before emerging in its modern form via the establishment of learned societies of architects in the late 18th and early 19th centuries. This model has proven surprisingly resilient, and remains to this day largely intact, although perhaps endangered.

These professional roots also illustrate the applied nature of the art of architecture; the fact that it is, and always has been, a business, something umbilically tied to commerce and indeed politics. The achievements of Leonardo, Borromini and Palladio would not have been possible without the patronage that supported them, and could not have been delivered if these pioneers had lacked the commercial and political acumen necessary to nurture such relationships.

Let's also take a look at other creative professions, from which there may also be much to be learned. The old adage has it that they don't call it show 'art', they call it show 'business'. Rare indeed are successful entertainers that have not spent long years travelling a circuit of small venues, working with challenging and discerning audiences. The ability to hustle, to tailor an act to suit different contexts and to critically evaluate performance is generally honed through a long apprenticeship on the road. Payment by booking makes the business element totally, indeed painfully, transparent to the emerging entertainment professional. An important key to success is having the right agent, with the right connections and the right sector knowledge. The role of the agent in show business illustrates the vital importance of effective marketing and public relations for creative industry professionals.

If the world of the professional entertainer requires drive, determination and dedication, then that of the professional fine artist is perhaps the ultimate illustration of the need to combine creativity with entrepreneurship. There can be no doubt that fine artists are part of an industry, which just like architecture operates across both the public and the private sectors of the economy. Paralleling the development of the architecture profession, the origins of the fine art profession as we currently recognise it also go back to the Italian Renaissance and the system of patronage by nobility and church. From this model has evolved the figure of the fine artist as a brand with which we are familiar today, driven primarily by the auction house market, but also to a not insignificant extent by the subsidised public art sector. The artist most associated in the common imagination with this transformation of high art from the system of patronage into the modern paradigm of the fine art industry is Picasso. Picasso was able to combine a capacity for endless innovation with an intuitive sense of the potential

//
In the end there has to be a profit motivation if a practice is to survive and thrive, and a comprehension of some basic business skills can be applied in many ways //

Tim Bailey

for the artistic person to be analogous to a product brand. The inheritors of this tradition are the familiar global names of the contemporary fine art world.

If the creative arts are a business, why is it often the case that little attention is given to the development of business skills during architectural education? Partly this must be a result of the need to offer education and training that meet the requirement for a broad grounding in arts, science and letters, while at the same time providing the emerging architect with the necessary core design skills that can only be acquired through many hours of studio work. Bluntly put, there is a hell of a lot to fit in. However, I am always struck that the schools of art appear to inculcate in students of fashion, fine art and graphic design a somewhat stronger entrepreneurial spirit than happens in a school of architecture. This is surprising, given that the practice of architecture is at least as, if not more, practically grounded in commercial realities. Maybe the harsh realities and fierce competition of art, advertising and fashion bring a greater pragmatism to bear and encourage an engagement with issues of business planning, marketing and promotion, communication, negotiation and financial management at an earlier stage.

That the business of architecture as it is now practised is so obviously an analogue for a form of market capitalism red in tooth and claw makes it all the more puzzling that architects are genuinely perceived to be weak in business skills and managing costs, and still seem reluctant to embrace up-to-date approaches to business management. Architecture is at the mercy of economic forces, whether they be interest rates, government spending policy or investment markets. Feast or famine is the nature of the game. In the long recession that started in 2008 and from which the architecture profession only began to emerge in 2013, aggregate workloads for the UK profession as a whole fell by one third.[13] And yet, the profession has an uncanny ability to fragment, re-assemble and rise phoenix-like from the ashes of each recessionary cycle.

Some of this reluctance to really think through the business of architecture probably stems from a form of professional identity crisis. In the 1960s the great majority of the UK architecture profession was directly employed in the public sector – in county architects' offices, central

13__Source: RIBA Future Trends Survey.

government departments, the NHS – supporting the great building programmes of the post-war social settlement in housing, education and healthcare, with well-funded teams operating beyond the confines of market forces. A small 'commercial' sector of private firms enjoyed a relatively protected market with a mandatory fixed fee scale. This market protection was balanced by strict code of conduct restrictions on marketing and advertising and provisions to ensure high ethical standards and the avoidance of commercial conflicts, so for example architects could not act as developers or contractors and traded either as sole principals or as partnerships, with consequent personal liabilities. Not surprisingly, architects were not immune from the revolution in market liberalism in the 1980s and 1990s, and gradually, following interventions first by the Monopolies and Mergers Commission and later the Office for Fair Trading, this highly regulated environment was transformed to the situation of today, where there is a free market in fees and relatively few restrictions in trade, with the great majority of practices trading as limited liability entities, and only a tiny percentage of architects working in salaried positions in the public sector.

The practice of architecture in the UK context has therefore moved from being a profession focused to a large extent on social programmes and with a strong sense of social purpose, which enjoyed significant employment protections in the public sector and market protections in the private sector, to being a free market model. To some extent the profession has in making this transition struggled to strike the right balance between the need to embrace business practice, commerce and competition and maintaining its ethics and sense of responsibility to society. This angst can be seen in the nuanced language that surrounds the business aspects of architecture, where the fear of being perceived as having travelled too far from the safety of *professionalism* towards the dark, uncharted and dangerous waters of *trade* is played out. Thus architects have clients not customers, charge fees not bills, proffer agreements not services contracts, and work in studios not offices.

Architecture cannot be realised in anything but purely paper form without a pro-active engagement with the business of development and construction; in other words, the industrial context of architecture. There can be no self-denial in this regard. An alternative might be to attain well-paid employment in the city, to marry into money, or to win the lottery; you can then design and build your own luxury home to your own exacting specification and to meet your own philosophical needs. If not, you are in the business of architecture.

//
First and foremost, I would define a successful building project as one with a happy client. Hopefully it is also a beautiful building //
Soraya Khan

11 ARCHITECTS CAN LEARN BUSINESS SKILLS

Studying architecture at university is usually categorised as undertaking a vocational course, and there is certainly a general perception that architectural education is oriented towards a viable professional occupation. Of course, in reality many undergraduate architecture students do not go on to become professional architects, but instead employ the critical and design thinking skills they have developed in a wide range of other roles, some of which are aligned or in proximity to the world of architecture and some of which are not. Nevertheless, the architectural education curriculum is predicated on the existence of a financially viable professional practice sector.

My perception is that students entering courses in other types of creative industry are perhaps more circumspect about the prospects for business advancement and the challenges they will face. Anyone entering the world of fashion, for example, is unlikely to suffer from an illusion that it is anything other than an arena where there is no shortage of talent and no lack of intense competition. This perhaps instils in the culture of fashion design courses a greater focus on the development of the necessary entrepreneurial skills needed to thrive in such a Darwinian environment. And yet the business of architecture is similarly financially precarious and competitive.

As an architect, it is important to learn about business as early as you can in your career, and there is no lack of opportunity to do so. This is not a suggestion to rush off to enrol on the latest MBA programme, but rather to develop awareness of some of the fundamentals that underpin the running of a successful professional services business, with regard to matters such as fee calculation, management and forecasting, profit and loss accounts, and cash flow forecasting.

The action of design is fundamentally about the designation of resources, and the architect needs to understand how to manage and most effectively deploy both the resources of the practice and those that the client is investing in the project. Thus an understanding of resource management – time, money, people, materials, energy – should be central to the knowledge base of the profession.

There exists a plethora of educational material about both the general business environment and the peculiarities of the business of architecture. Professional institutes produce regular surveys of the business performance of the architecture profession. For example, the RIBA undertakes its annual Business Benchmarking Survey and the AIA an annual Business of Architecture Survey. Close study of these types of documents will bring rich rewards for the emerging architectural professional.

// I would like to see the issue of managing resources – cost, time and environmental resources – taught as an integral part of the design process; as both intellectually and emotionally part of making architecture //
Sunand Prasad

What is an appropriate profit margin for an architects' practice? What should be the relationship between profit and turnover? How much turnover per fee earner does an architectural practice need to realise a sustainable profit margin? How much profit does each fee earner need to generate? What should the ratio be between salaries and business expenses? How much should a practice spend on marketing? These questions are not arcane, but rather address the nuts and bolts of what makes an architectural practice tick and work as a business. Gaining an understanding of these issues is essential if a practice is to function as a profitable business as well as a creative endeavour. There is no avoiding this; it needs to be embraced.

// Repeat work and referrals from past clients are critical to developing your business, so managing these relationships is a key concern //
Marianne Davys

12 ARCHITECTS HAVE TO SELL AND NEGOTIATE

Effective sales and marketing is a driver for all successful businesses. And yet, architectural practices typically underinvest in this activity, often leaving it to chance or serendipity. Data from the RIBA Business Benchmarking survey shows that architects' practices on average spend the equivalent of 1.6% of turnover on marketing activities[14] – far lower than other comparable professional services providers. While there are practices that take business development very seriously, in far too many cases marketing and promotion is left to those who, while they may be talented building designers, are least equipped to carry out such activity, and in the schools of architecture the art of selling is rarely a feature of the core curriculum.

In a desire to ensure that the veneer of professionalism obscures the more commercial aspects of their craft, architects of course, as we have discussed, have clients not customers, and furthermore they engage in marketing and promotion rather than advertising, but whatever euphemisms they choose they obviously need to sell: their buildings, their services, and most of all themselves. Perhaps one way of looking at it is that if the priest, the lawyer and the doctor are in the business of selling hope, then the architect is in the business of selling dreams.

Through the ubiquitous critique system, architecture students spend many hours at architecture school seeking to communicate their ideas and persuade others about the value of their designs. The obvious flaw is that these influencing skills are practised almost exclusively on people drawn from what Jonathan Meades calls the 'smugly hermetic milieu'[15] of architectural culture, which of course has its own internal value system and intellectual patois. There is little opportunity to engage with the vast range of humanity that might represent the clients, developers, funders and users of buildings, and so there is a grave danger that architecture students become expert in talking the language of their own profession but less practised in speaking the language of their clients.

But go to a lecture given by a truly successful architect and you will generally find yourself listening and watching someone who is an effective communicator and can reach out to a broad audience, beyond narrow professional confines. The architect may have succeeded through design virtuosity, intellectual distinction, specialist knowledge or ruthless self-promotion, but they will be able to put forward a message and more importantly covey a sense of the passion they feel for their work.

14__Source: RIBA Business Benchmarking Survey 2012/13.

15__Jonathan Meades, *Museum Without Walls* (London: Unbound, 2012), p.10.

If the skills needed to communicate effectively in the normal discourse of business and broader professional life are arguably under-developed in architectural education, then basic sales techniques are certainly not taught. Every car salesperson is grounded in the fundamentals of sales psychology and negotiating to seal the deal: first establish rapport with the customer, then point out the benefits of the offer, answer carefully any objections and concerns, then close things out. Such simple concepts about selling and negotiating rarely get discussed at architectural school, but just like the street entertainer, the market trader, the car salesperson, the priest, the lawyer and even the doctor, the architect has to sell, sell, sell in order to succeed.

It's helpful to ask yourself some fairly straightforward questions when trying to win or establish a relationship with a potential new client:

How much do you know about your client?
   What are their values, goals, aspirations?
   What is their track record?
   How much do you know about their financial resources?
Who will influence the decision?
   Who has the real power to make decisions?
What will add value to the project?
   What are the desired project outcomes?
   What do they really want? (This is often implicit rather than explicitly expressed.)
What type of fee arrangement is likely to be acceptable? (The client will probably prefer a fixed fee, but this involves greater risk for the architect.)
   Can you find an arrangement that provides assurance for the client while providing incentives for success?
   If the client asks for a lower fee, how will you respond?
Is the offer clear?
   Is it clear what is being charged and when it will be payable?
   Are the services clearly set out?
   Does the client understand what they are paying for?
What is the product that you are selling? (The end result of the process may be a building, but the architect is selling skills and services).
   What is the culture of your practice and does it fit well with the client?
   How are you positioning yourself and differentiating your offer in the marketplace?
   What is the key message of your practice?
   Can you establish an effective working relationship with the client?

The relationship between an architect and their client is not a short-term transactional interaction. Building projects inevitably have long gestation periods, and one of the architect's most obvious tasks is to persuade their potential client that they will be able to work well with them over an extended period, and that they are offering a relationship worth investing in. Often a building project can be an emotional rollercoaster: will you be able to ride it together?

In the context of selling and negotiating it is perhaps useful to also consider the matter of personal and corporate image. It is now conventional wisdom among those that write the most fashionable business-psychology primers that most interviewers have formed a fairly fixed judgement about the suitability of a job applicant within 30 seconds of meeting them. Clearly, right or wrong, appearances and first impressions do seem to matter.

//
The biggest barrier to establishing a practice in the early years is establishing credibility; persuading people that you can do it //

Tim Bailey

A well-organised and orderly studio will be reassuring to clients who are seeking security of delivery, whereas a more creative, stimulating and perhaps less controlled working environment might have appeal for a different type of client.

Among the RIBA's extensive collections are many portraits of architects assembled over 175 years of institutional history. In this treasure box are studies in oil of learned scholar architects in frock coats and waistcoats, grainy late Victorian photographs of stiff but steely-confident architects and their assistants in heavily furnished offices, gentleman architects of the 1930s in tweeds, sharp-suited and technocratic-looking architects of the 1950s standing in rows at high drawing boards, informal studios from the 1960s and 1970s with psychedelic clothing of the counter-culture and slimline telephones, through to more obviously managed and manipulated images of the modern media age. While these images to some extent simply reflect more general changes in culture and fashion, they also tell us something about the self-image of the modern architecture profession at different stages in its development.

It is clear that architects have always been conscious of image from long before the current media- and PR-obsessed age. Whether it is Sir Clough Williams-Ellis in spotted bow tie, plus fours and bright yellow socks, Sir Basil Spence in an elegant dinner jacket, Sir Hugh Casson photographed at work in an artist's smock, Mies van der Rohe in a muscularly cut suit with walking stick and large cigar, or Eva Jirnica pictured wearing a bold check jacket in a shiny chrome interior, all project a specific image of the architect, both as a type and as an individual character. These forms of self-presentation are able to embody powerful messages, as evidenced through the repeated use of the iconic photograph of Erno Goldfinger in bow tie and winter hat in front of Trellick Tower and that of Zaha Hadid in a suitably sculpted jacket, both favourites of picture editors.

While aspects of this commodification of professional service and self-promotion may at times feel uncomfortable, they are undoubtedly unavoidable elements of contemporary architectural practice at all its scales and in all its manifestations. After all, if you can't sell yourself, who will buy you?

13 WORK OUT WHAT KIND OF ARCHITECT YOU WANT TO BE AND PLAY TO YOUR STRENGTHS

The classic image of the architect is that of a Renaissance figure, balancing the knowledge of the arts and sciences that underpin the making of architecture. The profession itself has clung on to this model, generally resisting the idea of specialisation, and insisting in some senses that all architects are the same in terms of their professional knowledge and capabilities – a sort of general practitioner of building design.

Yet clearly all architects are not the same and the profession does in reality embrace elements of specialisation, whether by sector (commercial, housing, education, healthcare), skills (conservation, technical delivery, planning, design approach) or form of practice (large, small, multi-disciplinary, international, distributed, centralised).

Some practices trade predominantly on design reputation, while others might rely more upon quality systems, reliability and capability to deliver technical solutions. Larger practices can use their size to provide greater capacity and a wide range of services, while smaller practices can often offer lower overheads and a more flexible and personal service. Powerful individual personalities can be the main drivers of a practice brand, but there are also practices that operate very successfully on the basis of a more corporate, less personality-focused brand identity. Some practices operate across a diverse range of sectors, but others may develop their reputation through advanced knowledge of particular building types or building technologies.

Just as it is important for a practice to identify its unique selling points and where it can add value in what is a highly competitive marketplace, so the individual architect needs to work out what he or she has to offer that will set them apart, whether as a salaried employee or in developing a practice. For many architects the prevailing socio-cultural models within the architectural education system and the profession, which often portray the architect as a general practitioner who can operate in any building typology and as an individual artistic visionary, mean that the establishment of their own practice remains the ultimate goal. But this does not come without challenges or a price. Developing a client base is no easy task.

// It's a most amazing gift in life to find what you truly can and want to do //
Sunand Prasad

//
We try to build teams with
complementary skills ...
My advice would be to focus
on what you are good at and
you should progress //
Caroline Buckingham

For some the route of establishing a practice offers a creative and financial freedom and control that proves very satisfying, but others may discover reward in a more focused role within an established practice. Finding out and concentrating on what most engages you and playing to your strengths is more likely to lead you in the direction of an enjoyable and rewarding career path.

There is nothing wrong in recognising that not every aspect of architectural life is of interest to you or where your own personal qualities will best equip you to contribute. An architectural practice needs a range of different skills, and the profession benefits from being able to accommodate a variety of personality types and skill sets. Finding out where you best fit in this spectrum and honing your personal offer is an important first step in creating your own niche, and a key investment in your future career trajectory.

14 COMMUNICATE YOUR UNIQUE MESSAGE

What is special about you? What differentiates you from others? What can you offer that can't be found elsewhere? None of these are easy questions to answer, but answered they must be if you are to define your message.

One starting point is to think about those aspects of architecture that you are most passionate about. You are perhaps unlikely to make a successful and rewarding career in a small rural practice if you yearn for day-to-day contact with the beating pulse of architectural discourse and want to rub shoulders with the hottest new thinkers in the architectural firmament, but if you have a passion to engage with every aspect of the design and construction process from start to finish it may be the perfect niche for you. If you have an interest in the resolution of complex technological problems using the latest innovative materials and technologies, then working in a more risk-averse sector such as social housing may not be the best fit, but if you are motivated by societal and community issues it may be ideal. Someone who finds the inevitable and essential office politics of larger organisations anathema is unlikely to thrive in a large multi-disciplinary office, and yet for others the infrastructure and knowledge base of such an organisation may enable them to function at their best. If you are going to dedicate yourself to design aspiration in its purest sense and devote time to architectural competitions, then you might perhaps wish to spend the early part of your career working for and learning from some of the most respected design talents.

If passions are important then so are aptitudes. In this you need to be careful not to exclude undiscovered aptitudes for these may lie dormant, and no aptitude translates into ability and competency without first being revealed and then honed through many hours of practice and development. It is crucial, though, to make an honest appraisal of where your strengths may lie. At the same time identifying weaknesses can be helpful, for these can in fact conversely turn out to be strengths in themselves. An inability to articulate complex architectural theory

// It is an extremely competitive professional environment in architecture, and you have to stand out //

Soraya Khan

//
If you can find a niche that
interests you – say, passive energy
design or healthcare design –
and become expert in it,
then that can set you apart
from your peers //
Caroline Buckingham

in an academic context may mean that you are able to put ideas across in plain language, which serves well when preparing bids for work. A lack of strength in drawing may ultimately translate into the development of high-level skills using other visual media. There are plenty of notable architects with less than perfect drawing and writing skills. A lack of affinity with the soft skills of inter-personal communication and negotiation may come with a great ability to focus on research and technical tasks. Those who struggle with attention to detail may be good at grasping the big picture.

The idea of the 'elevator pitch', intended to encapsulate the concept of being able to put across what you have to say and what you can do in a few short seconds, has now entered the domain of cliché. Nevertheless, there is a useful kernel of truth in that when it comes to communicating your message, less often really is more. Learning how to express your unique selling points succinctly, in plain but convincing language, without resort to jargon, is a useful attribute. This principle can often be applied in visual material as well, when over-elaboration can confuse the message. As in a Lutyens drawing, what can be read between the lines may often be more telling and evocative than what is overtly expressed. A tendency to economy in communication is often welcome in the information-supersaturated contemporary world of big data.

Often to become special requires a degree of specialisation, so becoming something of an expert in some aspect of design, technology, business or sector knowledge is advantageous. Don't bury your knowledge in your own workplace, but make sure that you get out and about and tell other people outside your organisation, socially and professionally, what you can do and what you know. This will help you to hone and refine your personal brand and spread the word.

15 YOU NEED TO UNDERSTAND FEES

It's rare that two or more architects gather at a professional event without the topic of conversation turning before too long to the subject of fees. Just what is the secret recipe to calculate the right fee to win the job, while ensuring that it will enable the project to be properly resourced, deliver quality and value to the client, and at the same time provide a fair profit for the architect? Not too much; not too little; just right. When pitching for work and negotiating fees, how best should the architect set out the relationship between the services to be delivered, the resources and expertise required and the value added to the project?

Once upon a time, not so long ago, architects in most countries worked to mandatory fee scales based on fixed percentages of construction cost. Generally, as we have seen, the quid pro quo for this protected market was the enforcement of high ethical standards, heavy restrictions on the marketing of architects' services and limitations on areas of practice for architects: no activity as a developer, for example. Then in the 1980s a revolution began, as a more aggressive and confident free market entrepreneurism gained ascendency across the globe. In many places, not least the UK, it was decreed that the old cosy world of genteel private sector professionalism and public service paternalism was to be swept away in a storm of competitive efficiency. Oh no you can't, protested the architects, saying that their protected fee scales left little enough profit and scant protection from the ups and downs of a cyclical construction market. Oh yes we will, came the answer from many governments and competition authorities, and so the architects were sent out into the forest to face the big bad wolf of the market, and only the fittest would survive.

New challenges often bring new freedoms. For architects, the more significant of these included the option to trade as limited liability entities and reduce personal exposure to financial risk, the chance to experience the exciting new worlds of advertising, marketing, public relations and developing a practice brand, and the removal of restrictions on acting as developers. Exposure to a more competitive marketplace has brought commercial pressure on fees but it has also provided opportunities for innovation in services, technology, working methods and culture, and forced architects to adopt a more entrepreneurial mind set.

Architects have sought to find a path through the forest of market forces, balancing the need for enterprise and commercial creativity with a very real desire to hold on to cherished professional values and a commitment to the public good.

Each economic cycle inevitable ends in its customary recession, and the construction industry, so often used by governments as a key economic regulator, suffers some of the wildest swings from boom to bust. After each recession architects' fees never quite seem to recover to their previous level, but with much greater variety in the procurement methods used today and the corresponding services provided by architects, in reality it is almost impossible to compare today's apples with yesterday's pears.

So what are the main choices available to architects today to get the fee mix just right?

Put simply, there are three basic approaches to fee calculation:

Fees based on a percentage of construction cost
   The downsides of this traditional approach are that clients perceive it as failing to provide an acceptable degree of cost certainty and as offering little incentive for the architect to control construction costs; the percentages used are based on old historical models, and do not take account of the greater variation in services that are now commonplace; the only fee negotiating position is to offer a percentage discount – despite its mythical status, shrouded in the mists of a halcyon past, the percentage fee remains more alchemy than scientific method.

Resource-based fixed fees
   Fees of this type can be matched more closely to the services to be delivered and the value explained with greater clarity, and clearly clients prefer the cost certainty, but the architect takes the risk that their estimate of time/resources may be inaccurate. Successful resource-based fees rely upon accurate time recording of project work to build up a realistic picture of how long it takes a practice to deliver service elements on projects of different types. This can be a particularly difficult challenge for a start-up practice that has not had the opportunity to build up a database of project resourcing.

Hourly rates
   Hourly fees can be readily benchmarked in the marketplace and can be a useful option for more specialist services and for brief preparation and feasibility work (high-value activities that architects often give away too easily on a speculative basis when chasing new work), but they remain a very difficult sell for the main project delivery stages.

Too often architects undertake the crucial early work in strategic definition, brief development, feasibility study and concept design too cheaply, yet work for the RIBA report

// They never know when to stop designing, which can impact on profitability. For architects, design is a never-ending process //
Caroline Buckingham

// We try not to relate our fees directly to the construction cost. We now have a reputation for coming up with different answers, and we want our fees to reflect the value we add in this way //

Tim Bailey

'Client Conversations'[16] has shown that clients themselves recognise just how important these early stages are to achieving successful project outcomes. Indeed, research has consistently shown that it is generally the perception of clients that architects add maximum value at this formative stage of a project.

When it comes to fees, as well as the matter of *fee calculation*, architects also have to consider the issues of *fee management*.

Traditionally, invoicing of architects' fees was structured around the end of work stages (brief and preparation, concept design, technical design, etc.), but this carries significant risks for the architect, not least because it means extending a lot of credit to the client, which impacts on cash flow and places a lot of money at risk in the event of non-payment; so a monthly fee-invoicing regime is far preferable. The provision of a schedule of monthly fee payments across the project programme is an essential approach in effective fee management. It sets an expectation of regular and prompt payment, provides early warning of unreliable or late payers, and reduces the amount of money at risk.

It is not sufficient for the architect just to issue timely fee invoices; this has to be followed up with an effective fee-collection process. Standard appointment terms generally state that fees should be paid within 14 days, and yet many architects allow their clients extended periods of effectively free credit, clocking up huge numbers of debtor days and placing further pressure on their cash flow. It is not enough to agree the fee and issue the invoice; the fees need to be paid. Ensuring that the client knows what will be payable and when, and then following up to make sure that payments are made, is a challenging but unavoidable aspect of running a successful service business of any type.

16__*Client Conversations – insights into successful project outcomes (RIBA, 2013)*, http://www.architecture.com/Files/ RIBAProfessionalServices/ClientServices/RIBAClientConversations2013.pdf

Prompt and regular invoicing and collection of fees is the main lever to accelerate the speed at which money circulates through the business, maintaining cash flow and reducing the need for working capital; money needs to flow into the firm quicker than it flows out.

In achieving the right fee to support a profitable business, the architect has to learn how to deal with one particularly pernicious hazard: *commission creep*. This frequently occurs during the course of a project when clients change their aspirations and requirements, adding work to the scope of service, changing the brief or asking for the approved design to be amended. Clearly the flexibility to make changes is an important aspect of the design and construction process, but it must be managed through appropriate change control procedures, and for the architect this also means making provision for the charging of appropriate additional fees.

Architects are, of course, intimately familiar with the concept of *loss and expense*, in which a contractor claims the costs of additional work and/or lost time when changes are instructed during the construction period. And yet architects are notoriously reluctant to invoice additional fees in response to commission creep. The reasons for this are partly cultural. There is something in the profession's collective value set that promotes a desire to respond to the client's requirements and cheerfully accommodate change, but if the fee implications of such changes are not pointed out immediately to the client it can be difficult to recover additional fees if the commission begins to creep yet further at subsequent stages. Talking about money is often difficult, but the consequences of allowing unfunded commission creep can be significantly more painful.

Like it or not, the realities of time sheets, resource allocation, fee calculation, fee forecasting, working capital, cash flow forecasting, management accounts, invoicing and chasing debts

// Architects do want to be paid appropriately, but we don't generally take this element seriously enough in the management of our businesses, in my opinion. We are quick to complain about levels of fees and remuneration, but seem unwilling to do very much about it //

Satwinder Samra

cannot be avoided in the running of an architectural practice. Clearly, nobody becomes an architect because they really wanted to be an accountant, but at the same time it would be naive to assume that an understanding of financial management isn't necessary at every scale of architectural practice from the sole practitioner to the largest of international practices.

At the heart of every successful practice there needs to be someone who understands and can demonstrate where the practice adds value (otherwise you are just competing on price) and can calculate, negotiate and manage fees. It is unavoidable.

FOCUS ON PEOPLE AND PROCESS, NOT PRODUCT

The predominant pedagogic culture in schools of architecture is predicated on the primacy of process over product. In other words, the student of architecture is encouraged to emphasise the interrogation of design problems in an iterative process of exploration rather than seeking to arrive too quickly at design solutions, and indeed to provide evidence of this process through sketchbooks and working models. At a simple level, this can also be illustrated by modern architecture's general preference for asymmetry over symmetrical forms, since symmetry can imply a predetermined design resolution. However, in reality the finished output of a final design, as represented in drawings and digital and physical models, remains the most powerful expression of the architectural design process and is the most prominently displayed element in end-of-year exhibitions and publications of student work.

Clearly, an architect's output in terms of completed buildings, and indeed unrealised designs such as competition entries, is an important asset in competing for work, helping to establish the track record and professional credibility essential to reassure clients to trust the architect with their hopes, aspirations and, perhaps most keenly, money.

Let's visit the website of an architectural practice, where we will generally find a visually rich presentation filled with seductive images of its high-quality architecture, with all of the emphasis on the building projects that the firm has undertaken. Often these will be organised by sector or by building type; some of them may even be award-winning works of architecture. But the emphasis will almost invariably be on the product of the firm. There will perhaps be some shorter content explaining the practice's design approach and philosophy – rarely on the home page, though – and then, typically even more hidden away, a brief description of the key staff members, predominantly focusing on the buildings they have produced and their academic and professional credentials. Rarely do the individual personalities shine through with any great clarity.

// We perhaps don't talk enough about architecture being a service industry, which after all it is //

Kay Hyde

Now take a tour of some of the websites of the other professional consultants who fish in the same pond as the architect, typically the ubiquitous project managers and multi-disciplinary construction and management consultancies. Here the focus is likely to be very different. Pen portraits of the main directors and partners will probably feature heavily on the main pages, emphasising the skills, experience and personalities of the key players within the business. There may be content that sets out the working methods of the firm, the way in which they work with their clients and the processes they adopt. Client testimonials may be featured without any awkwardness, and an explanation of that somewhat nebulous entity: the culture of the organisation. Clearly, these firms believe in the philosophy that people buy from people.

We might pause to speculate as to why these two very different approaches exist within the same industry. I believe it is because the focus on product is very deeply embedded in the architect's psyche, even though the educational process is ostensibly focused on process. It is a profession that is proud of the impact its endeavours have upon the built environment and the benefits (economic, social, environmental and cultural) these buildings bring. The built output is the most tangible and measurable result of the architectural process, and the thing that makes all the blood, sweat and tears worthwhile. The other professionals involved in the construction of buildings perhaps lack the emotional attachment and commitment to both the process and the product that is both the blessing and the curse of the architect. However, this relative detachment from the product enables them also to recognise more easily that in developing projects it is people, the human element, that most influence the quality of outcome and the level of success. Buildings are designed and constructed for people by people.

From the client's perspective, the relationship with their architect is a relatively long-term business relationship; building projects take many months, often years, to move from conception to completion, with multiple financial, legal, planning and regulatory obstacles to be navigated along the way. The appointment of the architect and design team is therefore a far from simple transactional arrangement. Rather, the client needs to feel that the practice they are engaging provides them with the right cultural fit, and above all that the individuals with whom they will be working inspire high levels of trust and confidence. A client may well take for granted that a professionally qualified architect has the necessary knowledge and ability to deliver the creative, technical and management aspects of a project, and the more intangible elements that influence a successful client–architect business relationship may be of weightier concern in selecting the most appropriate architect.

//
Our architects need to
make a difference that
adds value to the project,
not just their portfolio //
David Partridge

// Clients want architects they can trust to deliver what they want, and who will be open if anything goes wrong. They are interested in long-term relationships with their architects //

John Assael

Different architectural practices have different things to offer in terms of their working culture and the personalities they bring to the project, and these less tangible aspects can be just as important to your potential client as more concrete criteria, such as track record, financial position and quality management systems. The types of architectural culture that might work well with, say, a creative tech company, a government department and a niche commercial developer are likely to be very different. It is essential that the architect is able to communicate these things effectively, and does not get too bound up in the product bias that characterises the profession. There is also a danger that in focusing too much on buildings as finished products architects do not emphasise sufficiently the importance of a rigorous design process and ensure that the client understands the need to allocate sufficient time and resources to that process. This is turn can lead to a lack of clarity about the value the architect brings to a project.

17 KEEP UP TO DATE WITH NEW TECHNOLOGY AND NEW THINKING

The pace of change just seems to increase all the time, doesn't it! Today architects are faced with the particular challenges of dysfunctional development economics, Building Information Modelling (BIM), off-site construction and sustainable design, but tomorrow it may well be different issues that preoccupy architects. Change is always with us, and the only constant.

Arguably, those who lived through the industrial revolution, or perhaps even the Second World War and its aftermath, saw greater overall social and technological change than current generations. However, in my lifetime there has been one area of technological development that has brought seismic change in business and society: the information revolution. From the microchip through the personal computer to the World Wide Web and the iPhone, the relentless progress of desktop, networked and now cloud computing has created significant change in both our personal and our professional lives.

The arrival of affordable desktop computer-aided design (CAD) in the mid-1980s, coinciding with the widespread adoption of word processing for the preparation of written documentation, was probably the single most dramatic business technology development to date in terms of direct impact on architectural practice. Up until then only the largest architects' practices could consider organising their design processes around CAD, which had been based on heavy-duty solutions adapted from the aerospace and motor-manufacturing industries. The emergence of the cheap and cheerful desktop computer enabled the whole architecture profession to migrate to a computer-based design environment, and you would be hard pushed to find an architect's studio today that is not an almost wholly computerised environment. The drawing board and Rotring pen are now items of purely nostalgic interest to mid- and late-career architects, and merely historical curiosities to younger generations.

While CAD offered clear advantages for saving time in reproducing repetitive elements on architectural drawings and adapting drawings to incorporate revisions and amendments, the overall efficiency savings it brought to the architectural design and management process are perhaps surprisingly small, arguably as little as only of the order of 5–10%. Nevertheless, CAD brought an immense culture change in the workings of architectural practice, and to be left behind in this rapidly advancing technological wave was to risk marginalisation at best and redundancy at worst.

The networking of desktop computers within businesses and externally through the internet, coupled with the reduction in costs of the parametric modelling and relational database software that enables BIM, is now driving a second information technology revolution in architecture and the wider construction industry. BIM is promoted by its advocates as a sure-fire way of promoting more effective collaboration in a notoriously fragmented and confrontational sector. It certainly offers the possibility of more effective sharing of data between the different members of the design and construction team, assisting collaboration and providing more consistent production information. The greatest gains will probably emerge when models are shared with specialist sub-contractors and suppliers, enabling true linkage of design and manufacture. The jury is still out as to whether these gains will be as dramatic as claimed by the enthusiasts, but we are certainly at the crossroads of a further technological paradigm shift – one in which an aspiring architect would not wish to be stranded on the wrong side of the incoming tide.

Generally, technological shifts of this type are advantageous to the generation of emerging architects because they are more likely to be aware of the true implications of these developments and to have the opportunities to attain the associated skills than their more established peers, who are often too preoccupied with running projects and businesses to devote time to the necessary learning and training. This is therefore an additional incentive to be on the right side of the rising curve of technological change.

There are any number of key issues, in addition to BIM, with which the emerging professional needs to be up to date. These include:

Sustainability and resilience of buildings – This will remain a hot topic for architects, and the demand for knowledge in this area can only grow. This is not only because of the increasingly ambitious carbon reduction targets that are being set by governments and regulators, but also because sustainability is becoming a core value in society, in the same way as accessibility and inclusion.

Off-site construction and prefabrication – This is emerging as a driving force for efficiency and quality control in delivery. It can range from prefabricated components including windows, door sets and precast concrete floors, through pre-assembled elements such as cladding units and structural insulated panels (SIP) and volumetric assemblies for units such as bedroom/bathroom pods and plant rooms, through to complete prefabricated buildings. It is said that 85% by value of the construction of

// All industries have to be acutely aware of both threats and opportunities. We can't afford to be old-fashioned in our outlook or trapped by tradition //
Caroline Buckingham

the 48-storey Cheesegrater building at 122 Leadenhall Street, London, by Rogers Stirk Harbour and Partners was prefabricated.[17]

3D printing – Recent developments in this technology have excited great interest among architects. The economies it has brought to model-making have seen a resurgence in the use of architectural models as a key communication tool for practices. It remains to be seen whether the use of these technologies can be effectively extended to enable direct manufacture of building components from the architect's BIM model.

The ageing population – In western Europe and Japan we are already beginning to see the impact on society and economics of a rapidly ageing population. This will have significant implications for the design of the built environment, so an interest in demographics may be more relevant to the architect's craft than is apparent at first glance.

Keeping up with these endless new ideas, issues and concepts is a challenging task. The architecture profession is fortunate in that it has been able to sustain a wide range of specialist journals and magazines, both print and online, which enable architects to keep their fingers on the pulse, and these are essential reading, but it is also important to move outside the architectural bubble. Magazines such as *The Economist* are good sources of information on the broader economic and social issues that inevitably impact on the world of architecture and construction. If possible, attend at least some conferences in the areas in which you are interested; developing specialist knowledge will put you at an advantage in establishing your role within a practice. In the world of social media, it is also important to make good use of the main networks such as LinkedIn and Twitter, which are becoming increasingly important sources of information in a professional context.

We are of course talking here about keeping up with today's technology and thinking, but while attempting to forecast future developments is beyond the scope of this book, it is important to stress that the real gains are to be had in being ahead of the game. Who knows what will be the implications for the future architect of developments in hand-held technologies, cloud computing and social networking, or what the inhabitants of Silicon Valley and Silicon Roundabout are capable of dreaming up over the next decade? And as we have seen, it is not just in the realms of technology that it pays to keep up with new thinking. The range of issues that impacts upon architects is as wide as that which affects the society architecture serves, and the world of ideas always impacts upon pragmatic realities in due course. In the decades after the Second World War those seeking to predict societal change in the UK usually looked to ideas from the USA as the most likely predictor of future trends. This is likely to remain the case in many fields, but what also will be the impact of ideas from other places in a world of globalised communications? Exhausting as it may be, we all just have to keep up.

17__Thomas Lane, 'The Cheesegrater: one for heavy metal fans,' *Building*, 13 September 2013, http://www.building.co.uk/the-cheesegrater-one-for-heavy-metal-fans/5059954.article

18 LOOK AFTER YOUR PERSONAL BRAND AND NETWORKS

It is only in recent years that architects' firms have really woken up to the value of brand. Traditionally architects' practices carried the names of the founding partners, or perhaps more daringly were acronyms made up of the initial letters of their names. Everyone in our consumerist society is now familiar with the power and value of brands, which today attach as much to individuals as to businesses and organisations, and architects are beginning to think much more deeply about what their brands signify to potential clients and what value they carry. Succession planning is notoriously poor even in successful architectural practices, and a brand that relies solely on association with individuals who may no longer be present within the firm in a meaningful way may have a limited future value. This is illustrated in the relatively low valuations assigned to architects' practices when they become available for merger or acquisition. Practices are now beginning to invest more seriously in brand identity, and we are seeing greater variety and ingenuity in the type of brand names utilised in the architectural sector. (One of my personal favourites is Square Feet Architects, based in Hampstead, north London.)

In an age of Twitter, Facebook and LinkedIn we are all also becoming more aware of our own individual presence as a brand. The ultimate expression of personal brand is reserved for those stars of stage, sport and screen whose fame is such that they are known by a single name, but we live in an age when everyone needs to actively manage their own brand in the context of their professional life, and this is particularly important now that any recruitment agency or potential client can utilise the net to find out about you or your practice from the (relative) privacy of their computer screen.

Having an up-to-date, accurate and informative LinkedIn profile is a good starting point, as this is often where people who have met you or heard you speak are likely to look, after a visit to your practice's website, if they want to learn a little more about you. There are then many online forums where you can start to engage in architectural debate, from Twitter to more specialised discussion sites. This is a simple way to start developing your own personal brand online. Of course, a cautionary note is needed – words and pictures once committed to the net are there forever, so be sure that you are happy to be publically accountable for everything that you post.

Make sure that you have a short, snappy and, most crucially, up-to-date CV, and that all your social networking accounts feature an economically written biographical note that explains succinctly what you have to offer in your professional field. When attending for interviews think carefully what you want your portfolio to say about you, where your skills lie and what your interests are, and be ruthless in your editing of it; make it easy for interviewers to see the very best of your work and to understand what you can bring to their practice. Become an

//

We get most of our projects through the relationships we develop with individual people and networks //

Shankari Raj Edgar

expert in some aspect of architecture and take every opportunity to speak, write or blog about that subject; in a world of electronically mediated communication there is no shortage of opportunities to find a platform from which to deliver your message. If you truly know your stuff, the more you'll be asked to do it again ... and again.

Just as architectural practices need to work out what defines them within the marketplace, so the emerging individual professional architect needs to discover what it is that they have to offer and how they are going to communicate this to those who can influence the development of their careers and businesses. This inevitably involves the development of a network of contacts. If you work in a larger practice, networking will involve developing relationships within your own workplace as much as outside it. While it might be nice to believe that all professions are meritocratic and that success is predicated on talent refined through relentless hard work, clearly contacts and personality also come into play, whether in business or in career development. It is partly for this reason that different industrial and service sectors – web tech, media and advertising, finance, pharmaceuticals, scientific research, legal, automotive – tend to cluster in hubs. There are advantages to being very close to your competitors. Here the movers and shakers can mix together, keeping a careful eye on each other, learning from each other and occasionally stealing each other's most talented staff.

Building your network really involves getting out and meeting people, whether that means taking out your earphones and moving away from your workstation to get some words of wisdom from an old hand on the other side of the studio or attending the best annual conference in your sector. It can mean simply joining the meetings of your local architects' society or the chamber of commerce or attending a continuing professional development (CPD) seminar. The trick is just to get out there. Remember that it is 80% about listening to other people (everyone's favourite subject is of course themselves) and 20% having something that you know a lot about so that you can tell others about it. It is rather like learning to ride a bicycle: a bit wobbly at first, but once you've got the hang of it there will be no stopping you.

19 PRIZES MATTER – DON'T THEY?

Many of us like to pretend that prizes don't matter to us. (This is perhaps especially the case when we haven't won!) Architects are by no means an exception: indeed, quite the opposite; there is a healthy market for architectural prizes, from the most internationally prestigious to the most specialised and local. Nearly every architectural institution worldwide or local architects' society runs some form of design awards.

The Aga Khan Award for Architecture, the AIA Gold Medal, the Alvar Aalto Medal, the Pritzker Prize, the RIBA Gold Medal, the UIA Gold Medal, the Thomas Jefferson Medal in Architecture and the World Architecture Festival are just a few of the seemingly endlessly growing list of international architectural awards, illustrating the ceaseless appetite among architects for glittering architectural prizes.

Conventional wisdom in the architecture profession is that prizes do indeed matter, and most awards programmes are hotly contested with plenty of willing entrants. Awards and prizes carry reputational prestige and represent tremendous PR opportunities, with coverage in the specialist and general media. They provide an architect with credibility and authority and confer design kudos. And yet it is important to recognise that prizes tell you about the current conventional wisdom and what the architectural establishment considers the gold standard to be now, rather than what the future will look like. You are surely more likely to learn about the future direction of architecture at a student exhibition than at an awards evening. Architectural prizes and awards are also generally judged by other architects, so they perhaps tell us more about what our peer group values than they do about the viewpoint of clients, funders and the wider society that we serve. It's that same old problem again that started in the first-year studio: talking to ourselves. In short, it's important to be clear what awards and prizes are, and what they can and cannot do for you.

Criticism (if constructive) is arguably of more use to the architect than plaudits. Criticism can be evaluated, weighed and reflected upon, and indeed ultimately rejected if it is found to be wanting. Criticism may offer some spur to future improvement, whereas praise brings only momentary satisfaction. On the other hand, success does breed success.

I once sat next to a distinguished and highly respected architect at an awards event and asked what had been the most rewarding aspect of practising as a successful architect. Without hesitation the answer came back: 'When a client understands and appreciates what you are doing for them and tells you, and more importantly the team.' What struck me most was that this reply could equally have come from a lawyer, a plumber, a nurse, a bookseller, a cleaner, a writer, a veterinarian, a cook or a doctor. It was a universal answer coming from the universal need to be appreciated and accorded some sense of importance. It was not

//
Winning awards is very nice,
but somehow endorsements
from your peers are not
quite as personal as reactions
from your clients //
Kay Hyde

in any way uniquely linked to the profession of architecture, but rather to humanity as a whole. This architect also instinctively recognised the need for this recognition to be for the whole of the team working in the studio, and the important role this played in motivating and inspiring them all.

Prizes do matter, then, because they represent a form of professional affirmation and recognition of excellence that has a clear value in finding future work, but it is important to remember that they probably matter more because they fulfil a basic human need for appreciation and leaving a measurable legacy. Awards and prizes are most important for those that win them and for the opportunities that often follow on. If you are trying to look forwards and see where things are going from here, though, to steal a bit of a march on your competitors, then there may be more fruitful places to go foraging. Every now and then you might want to ask yourself if prizes really matter.

20 CONSTRUCTION SOMETIMES INVOLVES CONFLICT AS WELL AS COLLABORATION

Much of the content of this book has focused on the value of teamwork, communication and collaboration, as well as the importance of understanding the role of architects and architecture within a complex project team and construction industry framework. However, the very reason that there have been so many industry reports and reviews over the years that have sought to encourage better teamwork, collaboration and integration in the construction industry (Latham, Egan, etc.) is precisely because it is by nature a fragmented and sometimes combative and confrontational environment, hedged in on all sides by legal contracts and liabilities, profit motives, professional turf wars, competition and regulatory complexity, and subject to extreme fluctuations between boom and bust. It would be disingenuous to pretend that the working life of the architect is one long love fest with supportive co-workers, appreciative clients, open-minded planning officers, consultant teams running with the precision of a Swiss watch, patient and generous contractors and delirious end users, all adding to the sum of human happiness. In reality conflict can, and frequently does, occur and the architect needs to be equipped to ensure that where possible it does not happen, but to be able to deal with it when necessary.

Most people dislike conflict; in fact, sometimes in our desire to avoid conflict we put off dealing with issues and this frequently leads to even bigger problems in the long run. In advanced capitalists societies we are by necessity highly individualistic and driven to pursue our own interests with a Darwinian ruthlessness, so some degree of conflict is at times almost inevitable. The inherent desire to avoid conflict is one of the biggest potential threats to the sanity and financial liquidity of the architect. The architect has an obligation to his or her client to make sure that they are informed about anything that may affect the time, cost or quality of a project. This is not to say that the architect guarantees these things – there may be factors that are beyond the architect's control – but that the architect must keep the client up to date about such matters. When a minor problem arises during construction, for example, the design and construction team may be tempted to seek solutions and to avoid incurring the ire of the client by troubling them with anxieties. Such a tendency is dangerous and to be avoided at all costs. Invariably such problems simply escalate, and by the time the client hears about them they have become more serious and the blame game may have already started between the various parties. Similarly, the architect may be unwilling to raise the issue of outstanding or additional fees with a client for fear of unnecessary conflict, or in administering the building contract may be reluctant to address poor performance by the contractor in a sufficiently timely way. Such conflict aversion can lead to a head-in-the-sand syndrome, which simply stores up greater future conflict.

The cut and thrust and commercial realities of getting building projects instigated, designed, constructed and occupied means that the architect needs to be equipped to negotiate with multiple parties. Getting past conflict and dealing with difficult people is never going to be easy.

//
There is plenty of hassle attached
to doing building projects;
architecture certainly isn't an
easy profession. Why do we do it?
That urge, desire really, to create
the very best buildings and
spaces is very strong //
Soraya Khan

You are likely to encounter stonewalling, hostile behaviours and even dishonesty. Successfully managing conflict requires keeping difficult emotions in check, finding some common ground and seeking solutions that are mutually acceptable. However, it is important to face the reality that these are difficult processes and that in this game it is not beyond possibility that at some point in your career you may find yourself in some form of formal dispute resolution process, whether mediation, adjudication or in court.

There are some straightforward areas where the architect can maximise the chances of keeping out of trouble. The importance, indeed necessity, of having a thorough written appointment agreement in place before commencing work for a client cannot be overemphasised. On commercial projects, watch out for some of the onerous obligations that can be introduced by lawyers and make sure that you do not sign anything that goes beyond the terms of your professional indemnity insurance policy. More than half of claims against architects relate to some form of negligence in design, often in the form of flawed or delayed construction information. Planning is also a significant source of claims. Traps to watch out for include inaccuracies in planning drawings (boundaries, dimensions, heights) resulting in the constructed building not being in accordance with the planning approval, and failure to ensure proper discharge of planning conditions and approval of materials. Architects also incur claims where there has been poor administration of the building contract. Areas for diligence include the timely processing of instructions, certificates and applications for extensions of time, and making sure that you have good management and record-keeping processes. As with the architect's appointment, there are real risks associated with projects that proceed on the basis of letters of intent, and it should be a priority to make sure that a formal building contract is executed. If you are involved in contract administration, make sure that you are familiar with the form of contract being used and keep up to date with developments in construction contract law.

In summary, deal with issues before they become sources of conflict and you may be able to turn adversaries back into partners; but make sure that you keep accurate records of all that you do just in case!

21 THERE IS NO ARCHITECTURE WITHOUT DESIGN

By this stage you might be wondering why, if all these things are so important to success in the world of architecture, they don't feature more heavily on the curriculum of schools of architecture, because they all do of course to at least some degree. The simple answer is that it is because, in the end, it is the core design skills in analysis, thinking and communication that are at the heart of what the architect uniquely brings to the building design and construction process. The game cannot really commence in earnest until the architect has joined the table and thrown a six. Although it is difficult to pin down the value that the architect brings to the process, there is no doubt that true value really is created on the sketch pad and on the (computerised) drawing board. The most ambitious engineers, cost consultants and contractors usually want to work with and be associated with projects designed by the best architects.

This central skill in design cannot be developed quickly, and so inevitably it tends to occupy the most time within the schools of architecture and crowd out some other elements. Arguably, though, some of the more business-related aspects of successful practice, which we have been considering here and which in reality impact directly on the design process, might be beneficially more directly integrated with design studio programmes.

The case being made that architects should not cede territory to others and should continue to maintain a broad range of skills and interests is not an argument for neglect of design and commitment to design quality in buildings. I would argue, though, that it is important for architects not just to mix with other architects, whether at university or in professional life. We should not be insular, but rather should engage with the broadest range of players within our sphere of activity: clients, developers, contractors, engineers, cost consultants, politicians, planners – the whole spectrum. We should not be afraid to understand and talk about resources; to design is to designate what should be done, with what, by whom and when.

If it all seems a bit overwhelming, we should not be disheartened. Architects may mature relatively slowly but they just carry on getting better. In a world in which big data and computerisation threaten the very existence of many existing occupations, it is hard to envisage an artificial intelligence system that will be able to automate the unique, complex and mysterious process that sits at the heart of the architect's contribution to society, culture and commerce.

PART/2

THE
INTERVIEWS

Part 2 of this book consists of interviews with 12 successful figures from the world of architecture, who have each achieved their own success on their own terms. In selecting a group of individuals from different types and forms of practice, the intention is to illustrate that there are a variety of approaches to achieving success, that success in architecture can be defined in different ways and that there is more than one type of successful architect.

01_____Simon Allford, *Allford Hall Monaghan Morris*

02_____Kay Hyde, *Hyde + Hyde Architects*

03_____Sunand Prasad, *Penoyre and Prasad*

04_____John Assael, *Assael Architecture*

05_____Marianne Davys, *Marianne Davys Architects*

06_____Bill Dunster, *ZEDfactory*

07_____Caroline Buckingham, *HLM Architects*

08_____Tim Bailey, *xsite architecture*

09_____Satwinder Samra, *School of Architecture, University of Sheffield*

10_____David Partridge, *Argent*

11_____Shankari Edgar, *Nudge Group*

12_____Soraya Khan, *Theis and Khan Architects*

01

SIMON ALLFORD
ALLFORD HALL
MONAGHAN MORRIS

Allford Hall Monaghan Morris (AHMM) is a London-based architectural practice operating at peak performance. Having established a reputation for an analytical and innovative approach to the design and delivery process, which they have applied across an impressively wide range of sectors and scales, they are now responsible for some of the highest-profile projects in the UK, including the master planning of the redevelopment of the iconic former BBC Television Centre and Google's new one million square foot London headquarters.

As one of the founding directors, Simon Allford combines his design and business leadership role at AHMM with an enthusiastic engagement in broader architectural discourse, through his work as a writer, critic, teacher, competition judge, design review adviser and commentator. Simon combines a sharp intellect and ability to think deeply and widely in developing design solutions with straight-talking directness that is refreshingly free from archi-speak.

He shares his thoughts on the way he has navigated his own creative and professional development, as well as identifying some of the pitfalls and perils he inevitably encountered along the way, and explains the qualities he believes the emerging professional needs to develop in order to find a niche in the world of contemporary practice.

Why did you become an architect?

I didn't make a conscious decision that I wanted to be an architect until I was 16. I had decided to do humanities subjects at A level, history and English literature and all that, and probably thought that my career would involve writing. Since my father was a successful architect (David Allford, Chairman of YRM), prior to that I had always thought that an architect was probably the last thing I would be; it perhaps seemed too obvious. I'd always enjoyed making things though, and at 16 I decided that the creativity I wanted to express needed to be about making, not just writing.

At YRM my father had worked on some big stuff, airports and so on. His was the bridging generation between the pre- and post-war modernists and the hi-tech generation. He had known some of the great figures of modernism, Mies and Aalto, so he was a tremendous source of knowledge. Once the die was cast, he was very supportive and over the years we had many conversations about architecture. I knew that I didn't want to work with him directly; I needed to plough my own furrow. He gave me support without trying to steer my career. He felt that his high profile might make it more difficult for me; that some people would want to help but that others equally might not. As a self-made man, though, he had innate confidence, and I think he transmitted that self-belief to me. 'Don't limit yourself' was his message.

What has been the single most rewarding experience in your career so far?

Architects tend to be self-sufficient. You have to believe in the value of what you are doing. Being a trusted adviser sometimes involves telling people things they don't want to hear – pointing out the problems. It might even mean doing yourself out of a job, perhaps pointing out that a building project isn't even necessarily the right solution. As an architect you are living in the world of ideas. You need to understand the people; the places; the city. You must not be arrogant, but clients do expect honest professional advice.

For me the reward is being involved in an endless engagement with making buildings and urban spaces. It is an ongoing process. It involves a series of journeys, working with talented people, and this is the reward in itself. I can't imagine wanting to retire. Being a valued adviser is recognition of your skills and expertise. At the start of the project I never want to say 'Let's do something like we did on such and such a project', but rather 'What should we do?'

Which skill has been the most important for you in achieving success?

At a pragmatic level, I would say the quality of perseverance and the capacity for hard graft. Then there is the 10,000 hours principle. There is the need to spend the time it takes thinking, drawing and writing to learn the craft. It is easy to underestimate the importance of the written word. It is essential to be able to communicate ideas in a clear, legible way. You mustn't confuse people.

What has been the most significant lesson you have learned from a mistake or something that went wrong on a project?

It is critical to always admit your mistakes and fully front things out when they go wrong. I remember a project where a floor of accommodation was missed out of a planning application – a simple, but embarrassing, technical error. We are still working with that client today. Honesty in these situations is crucial. Trust is everything.

What do you feel have been the hardest barriers to overcome in achieving your success, and how have you dealt with them?

Everyone faces the general problem of how many grey hairs you need before people will really take you seriously. But in the practice we find that younger staff members sometimes bring a perhaps more naive but also more questioning and searching approach, which is in itself of huge value.

A great deal comes down to how other people perceive your capabilities. Others need to have confidence in you and you therefore must have confidence in yourself. In general, potential clients and others make very quick assessments and it is difficult to change these early perceptions. However, you need to be true to yourself and not sell yourself on a false prospectus; you can't be a chameleon. A very softly spoken and considered person can be a convincing potential adviser just as much as a boisterous and sociable extrovert. You need to learn your own way of communicating and presenting yourself; to perfect your modus operandi. Relationships on building projects are quite long term, and different people will choose to work with different personality types. The very best project managers are those that can bring together a group of different people and get them to perform collectively at their best.

In identifying future leaders in your business, what characteristics and qualities do you look for?

A future leader needs to be highly committed and to have the skills necessary for design in the broadest sense – an understanding of buildings, situations and the working methods of the industry. These are abilities that transcend personality. I am looking for focus and passion for architecture. If you look after the creative work, your career will flourish, a career will emerge, but you will need to earn respect.

Out of the 20 or so most senior people at AHMM, all are very different; there are no 'mini-mes' or clones. We are looking for a balanced team. I find that the very best people are often surprised when they are promoted. Our future leaders often don't recognise the level of their own talent, because they are so focused on the activity of doing architecture. You need leaders, but this industry is all about collaboration and so the ego needs to be both expressed and supressed at different times. We very much have a culture of the best idea wins. We succeed by nurturing the best ideas, regardless of who or where they come from. Ideas get attacked continuously in a project, so those that survive have to have a core quality, an inner strength. Sometime such ideas can be incredibly simple – in fact they may not be overtly architectural – but they have to be tangible and robust.

What are your goals in architecture, and have they changed over the course of your career?

My goals haven't changed. There is a core sense of purpose, a strong desire to keep pushing forward so that the next project will be the best. Of course, only history will reveal if that has been achieved. I want to acquire architectural design and cultural experience. In one sense you are designing the same building over and over again, refining and improving your approach. The scale of operation changes but the core purpose is the same: the need to feel that it is essentially getting better.

You need to adjust your objectives to respond to opportunities as they arise. Don't view it as a tragedy if you lose out on a job; there will be reasons. Re-focus on the next opportunity, which may be transformational. Constraints and challenges are the mothers of invention. The next building might bring great leaps forward.

From your experiences, what do you think clients really want?

Clients want the architect to listen, lead and deliver. They want professional advice but not arrogance, so you have to be able to listen. They want you to offer vision, but that leadership has to be attuned to their needs. A failure to always deliver is the biggest weakness of our profession. You must match your promises; this is absolutely core. It includes working within cost and resource constraints. Others have taken over so much of our role because as a profession we have not lived up to expectations in these areas.

I think that architects have become less willing to lead. At one time the majority of architects worked in the public sector with a small private sector, but now we are all commercial architects. If the only thing you have to offer is design vision then in reality you are just a kind of building decorator. You need to be interested in the fundamentals of constructing and making, to be able to work in a team with the contractor, and to lead the whole process. Architecture is about operating at all scales, right up to 1:1. It might even include designing and making an improved contract to deliver the value in a better piece of architecture.

From your experiences, what do you think contractors really want?

The contractor wants competence, reliability of information and timely delivery. They will also enjoy the process of making architecture if the relationships and communication are right. Obviously the contractor wants to make money, but money underpins everyone's business. Arguably, money underpins too much of the contractor's interest and doesn't underpin enough of the architect's.

It is really important to engage the contractor with the design of the project. Give them the models, the CGIs; share the creative concepts with them as fully as possible, not just the production information. The vision needs to be communicated to the contractor.

What do architects really want?

For most architects what really drives them is the desire to build, to make. In the end it is getting buildings realised that counts.

What is the main motivator that keeps you going?

That the next building might bring great leaps forward.

Who has been most influential in helping you to achieve your professional goals and ambitions?

I have always resisted the idea of a mentor, but many architects have been a reference point for me. Not to ape them, but to try to really understand their thinking. How do they test and push their ideas?

The conversations I have had with my father have been a great inspiration and I think that I must also have absorbed a lot from him subliminally.

If you could add one thing to the architectural education curriculum, what would it be?

The fact is that there is no end to architectural education; you just carry on learning. The curriculum is just a passing moment. The boundaries between practice and academe are in reality very loose. They aren't concerned with different issues. Practice shouldn't isolate itself from architectural education. It is all seamless. If I could change one thing, I would break down the curriculum headings – design, history, theory, technology, professional studies and so on – because architecture is an integrated art. We are addicted to putting subjects into silos in the whole of our education system from secondary school to professional education.

What knowledge, skills and capabilities do you look for in newly qualified architects?

A broad engagement with architecture in its widest sense and manifestations.

A willingness to ask questions, but not the same question twice.

What advice would you give to a newly qualified architect looking to make their way in the profession?

Demonstrate that you are architecturally ambitious and show what you can contribute. Push that contribution, not your career. Find the right architectural culture in which you will flourish. There are many different practice cultures and you need to think carefully about where you can best contribute.

What are the most important issues that will affect the business of architecture over the next decade?

I think that we need to regain leadership, which is mainly about having the confidence to show vision. However, we will also need to rediscover a lot of lost expertise and recover the levels of trust by clients and others in the industry. We have let go of too many basic but core skills – working drawings, contract administration. The way we address this will fundamentally affect the future of the profession.

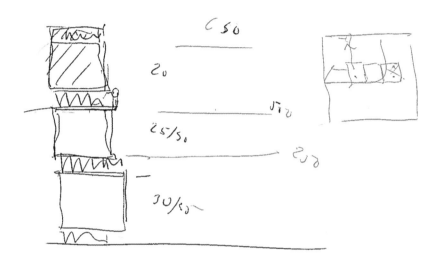

Study for a tall building as a suite of blocks both linked and separated by gardens

02

KAY HYDE
HYDE + HYDE
ARCHITECTS

Hyde + Hyde Architects, an award-winning practice based in Swansea, south-west Wales, has established a reputation for high-quality architecture, providing sustainable solutions, with a particular focus on passive strategies, through innovative construction techniques aligned with a rigorous, contemporary design philosophy and aesthetic. Kay Hyde, in partnership with her husband Kristian, works predominantly in the house and housing sector. At the heart of the practice's approach is the establishment of a very close working relationship with clients and a commitment to the highest possible quality of service and architecture.

After graduating, Kay worked for Hampshire County Council on education projects, then spent time studying and working in the United States, before returning to practise in the UK. Kay describes her commitment to achieving the best possible architectural outcomes irrespective of budget and other constraints, and explains her belief in the continuing role for an artisan approach to the crafting of architecture, as well as reflecting on the challenges and opportunities of being located at a distance from the traditional metropolitan hubs of architectural practice. She talks realistically and with insight about the central importance of the architect–client relationship in achieving high-quality buildings, and reflects on her search for the perfect client!

Why did you become an architect?
I suppose that every architect has their own story about how they found their vocation. Even as a young child I was very creative and very hands-on. My father was a carpenter, and growing up I was always by his side, helping to put things together. It almost seemed predestined for me to become an architect. I had a good sense of my strengths and weaknesses. Maths and art were both important subjects for me. When I completed a career matrix type test just before starting A levels, it wasn't surprising that architecture came out high on the list. I was very passionate about sculpture, and a career in art was appealing, but architecture seemed more vocational and perhaps more sensible.

Of course, the real job doesn't turn out to be exactly what you thought it would be. I can't spend all my time drawing; the administrative side that comes with practice has to be done as well.

What has been the single most rewarding experience in your career so far?
There are moments of excitement in the life of most projects when I have to pinch myself to check that it's real. When we are designing a house for a client and they see the designs begin to take shape – that is very rewarding. Clients put so much trust in you as the architect to help you unlock what they really want. If you can take those essential ingredients of the brief and put it onto paper so that they can really visualise it, for many clients that is a

revelation. Sometimes it can be quite an emotional experience for them. For many clients it is difficult to visualise things in three dimensions. We often make models early in the process to help with this.

Winning awards is very nice, but somehow endorsements from your peers are not quite as personal as reactions from your clients. There is something special about the one-to-one relationship with the client.

Which skill has been the most important for you in achieving success?

Communication skills are very important. You learn that people aren't always on your wavelength. Clients are sometimes reluctant to express their real desires and to give honest opinions, but we usually manage to break down these inhibitions. Sometimes if you feel that you haven't made a proper connection with a client, haven't really been able to pin down what they want, you have to go back to them and tell them that in a straightforward way and expand the briefing process further.

Now we have reached a stage when we can be a little bit choosier about our clients. It's better not to try to convert a potential client when you feel that you don't click and that you are probably not the right architect for them.

What has been the most significant lesson you have learned from a mistake or something that went wrong on a project?

Even when the relationship with your client is good, you have to keep working on maintaining the communication. There will inevitably be some ups and downs on any project, and it is a fairly long-term relationship with the client. People can get emotional, angry even. They are investing a great deal of time, money and emotion, and you have to just keep talking and working through the issues together.

I remember one of my Part 3 tutors telling us never to respond to difficult correspondence immediately, there and then, and that was good advice. It is important to pause and take time to consider your reply.

What do you feel have been the hardest barriers to overcome in achieving your success, and how have you dealt with them?

Although a lot is said about difficulties for women progressing in the profession, I have never personally experienced a significant gender barrier. When I was a young architect it was daunting going to site. The builders probably wondered how much I really knew about their work, but my strategy was to approach them on a basis of equality and ask honestly for their help and advice when I needed it.

In building the practice I think we had to overcome misconceptions about contemporary architecture. A lot of people think it is all about pristine white boxes, but good contemporary architecture can be highly contextual and elegant. We encountered similar issues with the local planners and planning committees in the early days. People would say things like 'We don't want anything futuristic'. Traditional architectural forms are very familiar and reassuring for many people, and to be fair there are some examples of poor contemporary architecture. However, as you get more established and you build more, it helps to break down these stereotypes about what architects and modern design can bring. Your reputation grows and a better understanding of what you are trying to achieve is reached.

In identifying future leaders in your business, what characteristics and qualities do you look for?

I recently attended a course on leadership skills in business. It was a generic programme, aimed at all types of businesses, not specifically architecture or design. One thing that was said that struck a chord with me was that an effective business needs people who can grow and adapt and fit into their role, so it is as much about personality, aptitude and attitude as it is about paper qualifications.

At one time we used to look purely at design talent, mainly as evidenced in someone's portfolio, but in a practice like ours the architects also have to be good all-rounders. They have to be able to deal with different types of people and be willing to ask questions and learn. Sometimes great design talent can come with a lot of self-belief, which is very dynamic and in many ways fabulous, but this doesn't always work in a practice setting, where you have to build up trust in long-term relationships with clients.

As we represent ourselves as Hyde and Hyde, we do find that clients expect to have direct contact with Kristian and me, because they are buying into a personal service in many ways. So this can be an issue to overcome when you are trying to bring on new talent.

What are your goals in architecture, and have they changed over the course of your career?

My fundamental aim is, and always has been, just to produce good architecture. Growth is not an ambition. Our model is in many ways an artisan approach. We are motivated to produce work of the best possible quality. The right work, the right staff – we are now a substantial way along the road to achieving that. It isn't really a capitalist model. I guess that we are trying to hone what we do, rather than broaden it in the pursuit of growth.

From your experiences, what do you think clients really want?

You do come across clients who have had less than perfect experiences working with architects previously. Clients want honesty and a good level of customer service. When you are designing and building houses for people it is team effort between the architect and the client. You have to keep close to your clients and ride the emotional rollercoaster with them. Some may never have been through the process before; others may be suffering a kind of post-traumatic stress from previous projects that have not gone so well. In the end it is about providing excellent service. We perhaps don't talk enough about architecture being a service industry, which after all it is.

From your experiences, what do you think contractors really want?

Contractors want and need good-quality construction information. We produce a lot of detailed construction information, effectively a manual on how to put the building together. The builder may only have experience of traditional construction techniques and we have to take the time to explain our approach. In our experience, contractors aren't stubborn; they are willing to listen to new ideas and try new techniques if you bring them along with you. Some of our local contractors have now worked with us on a number of projects, but we are also always working with people who are new to us. Many contractors are ex-trades people themselves and they are proud about the crafts they employ to build. When we introduce them to new approaches, this offers them new experiences that also have a value to them. We can offer opportunities for them to be involved in something innovative and of exceptionally high quality that they can use in securing future work.

What do architects really want?

We are looking for open-minded clients. It certainly isn't about having a fantastic budget, but more having a client that is on the same page. Perhaps we are searching for the perfect client. Sometimes you can take a client on a creative journey with you. They may decide to do something quite daring – it takes a leap of faith.

What is the main motivator that keeps you going?

Being in practice with my husband, Kristian, brings an intensity of dynamic. We inspire each other and bounce ideas off each other, so we motivate each other

Who has been most influential in helping you to achieve your professional goals and ambitions?

I don't think it is about individuals so much as the general architectural culture. It is always inspiring to see the work of good architects in the journals, and also to get out and network with other architects, which stops you feeling alone out there. We also both teach (at the University of Bath and the University of Cardiff), which helps to keep your ideas fresh. Architecture is never easy; it is hard work.

Being located in south-west Wales you can feel that you are a bit out on a limb, in a comfortable backwater, far detached from the metropolitan scene. In fact we are willing to take on good work anywhere, but there is a richness to our location here, working in incredible landscapes, which is a great privilege and very different to the urban setting of most architectural work. Our work is contextual rather than being routed in a particular place. We would like to work in a range of settings. Scandinavia would be a very interesting place for us to apply our skills. I suppose we are outward looking but with a strong Welsh core. There is a growing undercurrent of a Welsh architectural culture at this moment in time. It is quite competitive in a healthy way, we are pushing each other along, and standards of architectural quality are improving. We are all flying the flag for good architecture in Wales.

If you could add one thing to the architectural education curriculum, what would it be?

Architectural education is very ideas-driven. Sometimes I think that a bit more making would be of value, and perhaps getting architecture students to spend some time on construction sites. For many students it is a shock to the system when they first visit sites and they realise that when you are building it is not all as pristine and precise as on a drawing or CAD model. More exposure and interaction with contractors and skilled trades people would be useful, but at the same time you can't afford to lose the vision and creativity.

What knowledge, skills and capabilities do you look for in newly qualified architects?

Ideally, we are looking for people with some exposure to real building. As a Part 1 student you do need to be able to show that you can think in three dimensions. Making physical models is a good way to be able to demonstrate that. You need to have some drawings that are made by hand; it is difficult to assess artistic flair in computer-generated material. It is important to get as much experience as possible of all the project stages in the early part of your career – brief writing, design, the planning system, preparing construction information, work on site.

What advice would you give to a newly qualified architect looking to make their way in the profession?

Try to gain experience in a range of different practices, of different sizes and working in different sectors. There are a variety of different types of roles for architects and each practice is unique in some way. You need to work out where best you fit in. Sometimes we encourage students who are with us to move on and try something different so that they can get a broad experience early.

What are the most important issues that will affect the business of architecture over the next decade?

Our niche is all about preserving the art and craft of architecture, so I worry a little about the rush to standardisation that is sometimes promoted alongside BIM. We use BIM, and it can be very helpful, but I would be concerned about design becoming subject to multiple owners and adopting standardised solutions too early in the design process.

Sustainability is going to remain a major challenge, but we are moving into a more considered and informed phase in relation to resilience and sustainability. I am not sure that the push to go off-grid is necessarily the right approach. People are beginning to think much more about getting the basic design decisions right, and not allowing technological fixes to dictate things.

Architecture is a wonderful profession and there are opportunities for everyone. Some of the output of volume house building in the UK worries me. It is a mixed picture to say the least. Architects should be more involved in influencing the sector. The work that organisations like the RIBA do in promoting quality in housing is important. I also think that things like having *Grand Designs* on television has encouraged many individual self-builders to be more open to different design approaches. Overall it has been a positive catalyst.

There is a role for architects to become more engaged at the community level. We have a drop-in culture at the practice – lots of different people stop by in the studio for a coffee. Recently we have got more involved with cultural bids and events; we took part in the Cultural Olympiad in Swansea, for example. It is rewarding to do these things. It can open doors and people become more interested in your ideas and what you have to offer.

One of the first projects we completed as Hyde + Hyde when we set up the practice in South Wales

03

SUNAND PRASAD
PENOYRE AND PRASAD

A respected and admired architect, and an influential voice for the architecture profession, Sunand Prasad is co-founder of Penoyre and Prasad, an award-winning practice that takes a user-focused and context-sensitive approach to design across a range of sectors. Sunand has a strong commitment to the social dimension of architectural practice, and some of the best-known work of the practice is in the fields of healthcare and education. This sense of social engagement and concern with the needs and aims of clients and end users is core to the philosophy of the practice.

Throughout his career, Sunand has combined being a busy practitioner with a broad engagement as a writer, teacher and campaigner on professional ethics and architectural policy. His wide range of activities have included being a founding commissioner of the Commission for Architecture and the Built Environment (CABE), work on the development of the Construction Industry Council (CIC) Design Quality Indicators (DQIs), and being a member of the Mayor's Design Advisory Panel for London and the UK Government's Green Construction Board. He has been trustee of the think tank the Centre for Cities and of Cape Farewell, the climate change and art organisation. He is currently a trustee of Article 25, a built environment charity working on disaster relief and development. From 2007 to 2009, Sunand was the President of the RIBA. During his Presidency, he did a lot of successful work to focus the attention and energies of the profession upon the urgent need to address climate change.

Sunand explains how communication skills have been central to enabling him to place the needs of building users and communities at the heart of his design philosophy, and how the focus on providing buildings that really work for individuals, organisations and the public is a core motivator for him. He describes how the evidence for climate change and the need to move to a zero waste economy has meant that Penoyre and Prasad give environmental sustainability the highest priority in reaching design solutions. He also talks frankly about the need for architects to take on responsibility for managing time, cost and human resources more effectively as an intrinsic part of their stewardship of the design process.

Why did you become an architect?
My father was an artist, but although I enjoyed many artistic activities as a child, when I was at secondary school in England I wasn't encouraged to study art. My main interests were maths and physics, which were timetabled to preclude also doing art. I wanted to be an astrophysicist, a cosmologist. When it came to going to university, though, I went for engineering. I come from a rather political family and the idea of service, of being useful to society, had been instilled into all of us brought up in our Gandhian community in central India. I saw engineering as being an applied science that I could use to put values into concrete action and to do something helpful.

In reality, studying engineering didn't prove to be sufficiently nourishing. I used to look out of the windows of the school of engineering at the school of architecture next door and wonder. I was lucky. At the end of my first year at the University of Cambridge I applied to change to architecture. I was interviewed by Barry Gasson (architect of the Burrell Museum in Glasgow) and he accepted me onto the architecture programme. If I had applied for architecture first I probably wouldn't have got in!

First project, first term: I knew it was the right decision. It was the sheer breadth of what architecture could embrace; the integration of art and science. The RIBA Royal Charter defines the purpose of the Institute to be:

> ... the general advancement of Civil Architecture, and for promoting and facilitating the acquirement of the knowledge of the various arts and sciences connected therewith ...

It's a simple and accurate summation of the scope of the discipline of architecture.

It's a most amazing gift in life to find what you truly can and want to do. That for me is architecture. I have never considered doing anything else since I made that decision to change course. On the other hand, if being a rock god had been a real prospect ...

What has been the single most rewarding experience in your career so far?
I think that I am still really waiting for it ... you are always looking forward to the next project, the next challenge.

We have one client, a head teacher, who over a long period of time has continued to tell me what a difference our designs have made to the working of his school. 'The building never lets us down,' he says. There is a special reward in knowing that you have got things right in terms of the building as it is actually experienced by users. Often there is a buzz on the opening day, but what matters is the feeling years later. This was a large school, and we had tried to create an environment that would work for everyone in a community of 1,700 people, with places where students could gather in small groups, places where the whole school could come together as a community, and places where individuals could be alone and quiet. Knowing that we achieved that and that it had really worked to create that crucial sense of community gives a very positive feeling.

Which skill has been the most important for you in achieving success?
For me personally it has been the ability to work well with people. Of course, you need core design skills. The client wants your expertise, which is the most precious thing you have to offer; but unless you can communicate your expertise it remains locked up.

At the moment I feel that as architects we have plenty of professional expertise, but that we are not strong on communication skills. It is also important to remember that communication is a two-way process. You have to be able to receive and absorb as well as present information. At the heart of architectural endeavour there is a synthesising skill of putting things together. This is our unique asset: the ability to turn diverse inputs into a coherent whole. There is no one else in the design and construction team who can do it, and the rest of the team want the architect to bring things together and to offer that leadership.

There are two elements to this synthesis that have to be achieved. The first is process synthesis. What is the right sequence? What must happen and when? To do this effectively you need to understand the discipline of working with time, cost and human resource constraints, which is something we don't really learn in architecture school. The second is design synthesis. How do you make a design that is coherent in the context of the complexity of constraints and influences? There is a lot to deal with: spatial adjacencies, services, comfort, aesthetics and so on. We can summarise it under the headings of the Vitruvian triad – firmness, commodity and delight.

While process synthesis is something architects can learn, the person doing it in a team does not have to be an architect. However, it is more difficult without an architectural background to synthesise design in the round, to have the overview, to nurture the big picture. There are so many things competing to be the determinant parameter. A successful architect needs to have the ability to see through this confusion and communicate clarity of vision. It may be tacit, but you do need it.

The concept of play is important in achieving the balance between reason and imagination that good design needs. Over-reliance on rationality produces boring solutions, but over-reliance on imagination can result in failure of performance. The act of play can help to resolve these tensions. Doodling and sketching, they can be a form of play. Asking 'what if?' It's the act of taking a thought for a walk. Aalto talked about this. It has been called the ludic principle, after the Latin for play. Mark Dodgson, David Gann and Ammon Salter have really interesting things to say about this way of evaluating options and achieving innovation in their book *Think, Play, Do*.[1]

What has been the most significant lesson you have learned from a mistake or something that went wrong on a project?

I hope I have learned that you should always strive to do what you believe is right. There are times, I think, when I should have pushed harder, forced things a bit more the way I felt they ought to be. My regrets are about the occasions when due to circumstances, lack of time or resources I have stopped short. Such expediency tends to happen more as your practice gets larger, and it can result in compromises.

It is important to work with the very best people you can. You need the right mix of complementary skills in your team. There were times when I didn't quite get that mix right. You need the right team for the circumstances in order to succeed.

What do you feel have been the hardest barriers to overcome in achieving your success, and how have you dealt with them?

Winning the confidence of potential clients is a significant challenge. Many people can't see what is difficult about architecture. They can perceive the expertise and skill in the law, medicine, engineering, fine art even. Architecture doesn't seem mysterious or technical; perhaps only the cognoscenti really understand the mystery of architecture. So you have to be able to get under the skin of your clients and find out what they really need. If you can generate ideas that directly address those needs then you will gain their confidence and they will value your role.

01__Mark Dodgson, David Gann and Ammon Salter, *Think, Play, Do* (Oxford: Oxford University Press, 2005).

In identifying future leaders in your business, what characteristics and qualities do you look for?

There definitely are qualities specific to leadership. Good leaders have the ability to get the best out of other people; to get them to perform at their top level. Future leaders tend to be self-directed, to be able to work with a degree of autonomy. In reality they emerge rather than being discovered or talent-spotted.

What are your goals in architecture, and have they changed over the course of your career?

My goals haven't changed, but the times and the context for the practice of architecture have. Our mission statement, if you like, remains to make beautiful buildings that work for people. There may be things to admire in some strong ugly buildings, but I don't want to build them! Beauty has of course a lot of subjectivity. I look out of our studio window at the Barbican towers, an archetype of what most people think of as British brutalist architecture. To me these towers are beautiful, with the timeless quality that is the hallmark of great architecture. I aspire to that.

Sustainability, the pursuit of low energy, low carbon buildings, is a key concern for our practice. We had that from the start, and for me it links to my early upbringing in a community that pursued ideals of self-sufficiency, which are related to sustainability.

From your experiences, what do you think clients really want?

There are some common themes in the very different things clients want. They do want from the architect the most effective result possible for the resources they are investing in the project. They want you to manage both the possibilities and the resources. Each combination of client and project is unique. Some clients are more generous and inclusive; some are less open to wider possibilities. A lot of clients don't necessarily know exactly what they want. It is the architect's job to help them find out.

From your experiences, what do you think contractors really want?

Contractors want profit but also reputation. Most don't want profit at the expense of reputation. Beyond that it is difficult to generalise. Everyone will agree that accurate design and construction information delivered in time is a key to a good working relationship with a contractor. But that should merely be the basis. Contracting is changing and is no longer about just delivering what someone has designed and specified. It is important to integrate the contractor into the team. You need to understand the specific motivators of the particular individuals as well as the organisations that make up that project team and try to achieve alignment with the overall goals of the project.

What do architects really want?

Architects want the opportunity to perform and make their contribution to the built world, and to be recognised for it, while making a living. They want a chance to show what they can really do, to produce their own *Babette's Feast*.[2]

Today there is a mismatch between the way the architecture profession and education is configured and the opportunities for practice. The opportunities are no longer

02__*Babette's Feast* (1987), Danish language film directed by Gabriel Axel, based on a short story of the same title by Isak Dinesen (pen name of Karen von Blixen-Finecke) in the collection of tales *Anecdotes of Destiny* (1958).

available in the way in which the profession wants them to be and for which the profession was organised. We need to become in tune with the times but many of us find that difficult, probably including me.

What is the main motivator that keeps you going?

It is the only way I know to make my living! But beyond that there is a great reward that comes from feeling that you have made a real difference in people's lives and experience, that you have brought something of the new to them; and I have the conviction that I can carry on doing that.

Who has been most influential in helping you to achieve your professional goals and ambitions?

Ted Cullinan – I served the best apprenticeship I could have ever wanted.

If you could add one thing to the architectural education curriculum, what would it be?

I would like to see the issue of managing resources – cost, time and environmental resources – taught as an integral part of the design process; as both intellectually and emotionally part of making architecture. These are vital and compelling issues that architects should be equipped to deal with. When these issues are addressed in education it is generally done in a glum and worthy way, but they can be exciting parts of the design process.

Architects should master both form and resource.

What knowledge, skills and capabilities do you look for in newly qualified architects?

A genuine enthusiasm for architecture in its broadest sense is the most important thing for a newly qualified architect. They also need an ability to learn, which is very close to an ability to communicate and listen.

What advice would you give to a newly qualified architect looking to make their way in the profession?

Take some time to really think about what it is that you want to do. If you aren't enjoying what you are doing for any significant period of time then that particular thing is not right for you. It is also important to know your worth, but in an honest, self-analytical way.

What are the most important issues that will affect the business of architecture over the next decade?

Architects continue to find it difficult to place an accurate value on their work. The profession of architecture is based upon a set of principles and ethics, and if demonstrating value is not part of your professional eco-system then you will undervalue what you do. The market for architecture as pure art is very small, so we need to understand better where we add value and how we can demonstrate it.

Climate change remains the biggest single challenge. We need to shift to a zero waste economy. This will have a profound impact on the practice of architecture. Relationships, the resources and technologies we use, the appearance of the buildings we design – all will change. Architecture is both about the effective use of resources and an expression of our collective sense of self as a society.

Unless the Intergovernmental Panel on Climate Change (IPCC) is completely wrong in its assessments, this shift is inevitable. Human beings are ultimately survivors so we will eventually adapt to climate change, bringing about a significant shift in how we do things. Architecture is always enmeshed in the big societal issues; subject to them and an essential part of the solution. So architects will have their role to play in this great adaptation.

Sketch for medical research building

04

JOHN ASSAEL
ASSAEL
ARCHITECTURE

John Assael is the Chairman and co-founder of Assael Architecture, an AJ100 practice with a reputation for professionalism and a consistent quality of output balanced with commercial astuteness. With over 30 years of experience in his own practice, John has a particular interest in designing mixed-use schemes in urban areas. He has a Masters in urban and regional planning and a postgraduate diploma in conservation studies from the Architectural Association and enjoys working on projects involving important listed buildings and in conservation areas.

Very committed to supporting the values and community of professionalism, while running a busy practice, John has also dedicated time to a great deal of activity for the RIBA and the ARB as well as the Association of Consultant Architects, and he is a trustee of the Architects Benevolent Society.

With candour and insight, John tells us about his own journey in establishing and growing a significant practice, and explains how excellence in managing client relationships and delivery of service is at the heart of his business model. He sets out his own design ethos, which aims for consistency of quality with a focus on longevity rather than fashion, and explains why that commitment to quality has lead him to eschew the more simplistic forms of design and build procurement wherever possible in favour of more sophisticated approaches. He also explains why being a good employer and promoting good ethics is so important to him personally and so beneficial to the practice. John also offers some keenly observed comments on areas where the current architectural education system might update its methodologies.

Why did you become an architect?

I didn't have a burning ambition from a very young age to be an architect. In fact I didn't decide to study architecture until after I had completed my A levels and I wasn't sure that I wanted to be a practising architect even after I had completed my undergraduate architecture course. I have an identical twin brother and he became a property lawyer, and I think that I could also easily have gone off in a different direction to architecture.

After I had completed my Part 3 my career had its ups and downs. I was made redundant and I was fired from one job. By the time I was in my late 20s some of my friends who had gone into the law and advertising were really flying, making plenty of money and getting ahead. I seriously considered stopping architecture and trying my hand at something else. I probably established my own practice at too young an age; I was 28. I set up with a friend who had studied with me and we started two small offices, one in London and one in Bahrain, but that venture fizzled out. In my mid-30s I decided to really commit to building my own practice up. I thought: 'Yes, I will really make this work through my own effort and a huge commitment'; I was happy to put my own name above the door.

What has been the single most rewarding experience in your career so far?

In early 2014 we regained our place on the *Sunday Times* '100 Best Small Companies to Work For' list. This is for businesses with 50–200 staff. In the teeth of the recession in 2009 we were forced to make quite a lot of redundancies, and this meant we were no longer eligible for inclusion in the *Sunday Times* list because we had shrunk below the 50 staff threshold. Making a return to the list was a sign that we had weathered the storm and we were really back. We are still doing great work for great clients and are people-centred. We haven't lost our identity and our values remain intact.

I like to think that our practice has a different model. We want to be stable, care for our staff, offer a high quality of service and be consistent in our design approach, but not to be driven by fashion.

Which skill has been the most important for you in achieving success?

I would say that one skill and one attribute have been essential to my success.

The skill is the ability to get on with people and gain enjoyment from working with others. This is what has enabled me to get clients and keep clients; to get good staff and keep them. It means that you can work with the whole range of people involved in the process from planners to sub-contractors.

The attribute is tenacity, which I see as a determination to see things through. I just keep going even when there are wobbles along the way.

What has been the most significant lesson you have learned from a mistake or something that went wrong on a project?

Everyone learns some lessons the hard way. You have to collaborate with other people when things go wrong and enlist their support. Don't hide problems; be open; get your best friends and advisers around you. Be honest and behave well.

Earlier in my career I once designed a staircase that didn't work, and the builder built it the way I had drawn it just to make a point; there wasn't enough headroom. When I asked him why he had done it he simply said, 'Well, you keep telling me that all the drawings are perfect and that is how you want it.' I certainly had learned a lesson. Don't be arrogant, and learn from the builders. You need their help.

Things go wrong in businesses as well as on individual projects. At the height of the recession we had to make quite a lot of redundancies: 17 in one day. We had to talk it through openly with everyone, and a team handled the conversations with the individuals. It is an incredibly painful thing to have to do, and you need to share the burden and work together, not leave it to one person.

What do you feel have been the hardest barriers to overcome in achieving your success, and how have you dealt with them?

I haven't encountered any specific barriers. Although I established my practice at a very young age, I didn't experience barriers related to youth or inexperience. My wife and family have been incredibly supportive.

A number of my close friends also run practices, and many stay at a smaller scale, say fewer than 20 staff. I feel, though, that a slightly larger scale of business gives you access to bigger, more interesting projects. I do want to build a legacy, something sustainable, and to leave behind a team with solid client relationships. Some practices are just a flash in the pan. Some people want to build up a practice and then retire and aren't so interested in what follows on. I hope that our core people will carry on and that the values will stay the same – a trustworthy and respected practice.

In identifying future leaders in your business, what characteristics and qualities do you look for?

I interview every member of staff that we are considering taking on. It is madness really, and I should trust it to my colleagues, but I can't help myself. Getting the right team is so important. I look for certain characteristics. Firstly intelligence, but that doesn't necessarily mean a first-class honours degree; it could be good A levels. They need to be interesting. If someone is an Olympic sailor, then they might not be able to focus everything on their degree outcome. We are very persuaded by people who can demonstrate excellence in sport or music, because this shows an ability to work in a team. A commitment to charity work is also a good indicator for us – perhaps a gap year well spent. We aspire to a culture of giving something back.

Our future leaders need to be determined; to have the desire to grow and develop. Honesty is very important. They need to be able to admit to their mistakes and be transparent, not secretive.

What are your goals in architecture, and have they changed over the course of your career?

My goals have probably changed a bit over time. When I first got the practice going I would take on almost any type of work, because I was hungry to grow the business. Now we are more focused. At one time I considered going multi-disciplinary and widening our offer, but today I actually want to get more focused. The goals in our mission statement are:

We just do architecture.
We don't implement or deliver other architects' work.
We produce high quality work that lasts, and is not fashion driven.

Our architecture is often quite quiet. We aren't big advocates of lots of colour. We want our work to have longevity. I don't want the practice to be dominated by a single or a small set of personalities. As you get bigger, you have to bring in more people who are committed to the overall ethos. We are like an orchestra.

From your experiences, what do you think clients really want?

Clients want architects they can trust to deliver what they want, and who will be open if anything goes wrong. They are interested in long-term relationships with their architects. We care deeply about how our clients experience our services and how they perceive us. We commissioned a survey to find out what clients, contractors, journalists and peers think about us as a practice. It was expensive, but it was money well spent. Now we have got lots of real data. You can't assess your own reputation.

All of our team are important in establishing a good relationship with clients. How they interact with them on a day-to-day basis, how they conduct themselves, whether they meet deadlines. This is what determines the client's experience.

From your experiences, what do you think contractors really want?

Most of our work, certainly for major house builders, is procured through a form of management contracting, so we mainly interact with sub-contractors. What they want above all else is accurate information. They also need us to be flexible to their needs in meeting progress and cost targets, and to be quick to respond.

We are making increasingly sophisticated use of BIM in our provision of construction information. It helps you to identify the potential gaps between the different work packages. Things like fire and acoustic separation elements, which can fall between cladding and dry lining packages.

In the past we have done some more conventional design and build, but we don't enjoy the process. There is a tendency for contractors to look for short cuts, and trying to maintain quality is very challenging. I am concerned that with some contractors there is an increasing gap in values and knowledge between the skilled people who do the real work and the managers.

What do architects really want?

Respect and recognition: architects are sensitive creatures; they need a 'Well done' every now and again. I don't think architects are really motivated by money. It is nice, and we all have the rent to pay, but for most architects it is about recognition from clients and contractors and the wider public that they are making a valuable contribution to help make the world a better place.

What is the main motivator that keeps you going?

For me it is about looking after the team in the practice and providing the best possible service to our clients and partners. I enjoy the relationships with people and being a catalyst to make change. We are always appointed to be the architect and lead designer, and enjoy managing the whole process.

Who has been most influential in helping you to achieve your professional goals and ambitions?

I am not inspired by a particular approach to architecture or a follower of a specific architect or theory.

My identical twin brother is a property lawyer, and his counsel and advice have been very valuable to me. We help each other. I think that he has very much influenced the way in which I run the business and I have influenced the way he works with people. In some ways the practice is modelled a bit like a small law firm. There is a design ethos, but this is done with a light touch. My brother and I talk a lot about the businesses: managing people, winning clients, legal aspects. I have also been able to help him understand more about the buildings he deals with in his work.

If you could add one thing to the architectural education curriculum, what would it be?

I would add more about practical business skills. Personally, I am passionate about going out to the schools of architecture and lecturing about what it is like to actually run a practice as a successful business.

Overall architecture is a very tough course. Many tutors feel that you have to break the students down before you can build them up as effective architects. I think that it is a bit too harsh; it could do with a bit more love and support. The unit teaching system has some drawbacks. It is too much subject to the vagaries of the tutor. It is a bit subjective and image-obsessed, which I think makes it somewhat flawed.

What knowledge, skills and capabilities do you look for in newly qualified architects?

For me the portfolio is not of primary importance. I am interested in the raw material of the person. Do they have intelligence and tenacity? Can they get on with other people? Also, I am not so bothered about their existing computer skills. I am keener that they can be team players and can contribute. Do they have some experience of working in teams? That is where experience in sport, music or charity work can be so valuable. We want our staff to

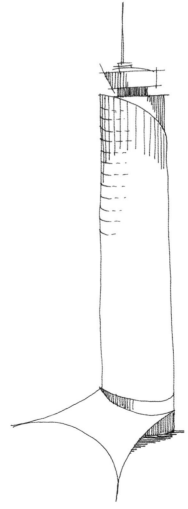

A sketch of The Tower at GWQ, West London's tallest apartment building

continue those interests as well. We have a band in the office and five-a-side football teams. When people are doing their Part 3 exams they sometimes need to dedicate a lot of time to that outside working hours, but when they emerge the other side we like to encourage them to rekindle their other interests and find a more balanced life.

What advice would you give to a newly qualified architect looking to make their way in the profession?

A commercial lawyer will say I aspire to be a partner rather than I want to set up my own firm. I would say to young architects who think that striking out on their own must be the ultimate goal, just park that thought for a little while and consider joining a practice where you fit well and build a career there. Two thirds of start-up practices don't succeed. You could be a very valuable part of a fantastic organisation. I think there is too much emphasis on the *starchitect* model. Not every pub singer is the next rock star. It is possible to develop in the profession within an existing practice. There could be a bit more emphasis on the collaborative nature of getting buildings built. In the end, there are only a limited number of opportunities to create the one-off, iconic works of architecture, and we need to make sure that the general quality of the buildings we produce is high.

What are the most important issues that will affect the business of architecture over the next decade?

In the British context, we are seeing a growing polarisation between the medium and larger practices and the rest. Very small practices sometimes lack resources and financial muscle and resilience, which I think makes many such practices vulnerable. There are some very low levels of remuneration out there. This doesn't happen in medicine, for example. A GP is remunerated at roughly the same level regardless of whether they are in a small or a large medical practice or where they are located. It is possible to grow a small practice into something bigger, and there is more security in being in the mainstream. There are some other models that can be tried, like federations of smaller practices.

Overall, the big factor that will affect the business of architecture is the state of the general economy; architecture is always subject to 'boom and bust'. Although we are now in a new growth phase, it looks as though the levels of economic growth we will achieve in the coming years will be somewhat less than we have grown used to. Perhaps we will be increasingly looking to developing work overseas.

05

MARIANNE DAVYS
MARIANNE DAVYS
ACHITECTS

While the ultimate goal for some architects may be to become a senior player in a large practice, Marianne Davys is an architect who, following a broad experience in metropolitan private practice as well as large public sector organisations, has found success as a sole practitioner. From her clean-lined and spacious home office in Muswell Hill, Marianne has a portfolio of high-quality projects across London: mainly residential, many involving works to listed buildings or in sensitive conservation area contexts, but also including commercial and school projects.

The success of Marianne's practice is built on a high level of quality in design and organisation in delivery, with a focus on developing strong working relationships with both clients and contractors. Marianne describes how her experience in small practice has brought special rewards in terms of engagement with design issues every single working day and being able to plan her working time to strike an appropriate work–life balance.

Why did you become an architect?

As a teenager in Ireland, I originally thought about becoming a Montessori school teacher, but then an architect and former pupil came and gave a talk at my secondary school and I, along with my classmate Sharon O'Grady, was hooked. We both became architects. The ugly, cheap buildings being erected in Dublin during the late 1960s and early 1970s, with total disregard for the impact on their setting, were also an important factor – I thought I could design much nicer buildings!

The idea of travelling and working in other countries was important to me, and I thought that being an architect might make this possible. For my final exams at secondary school I studied maths, art and five languages, so I was destined to be an architect on the move. In fact I have worked as an architect in Spain, Italy and France, so I did get to travel.

What has been the single most rewarding experience in your career so far?

I had already visited Venice during my time as a student and really wanted to study and work in Italy. Being awarded a scholarship by the Italian Culture Institute and spending three years in Florence studying the restoration of historical centres and buildings and working as a simultaneous translator on the same course was the most wonderful opportunity and was also where I met my husband. Later, working in an Italian architectural practice was a great experience.

During my time in Italy, I was fascinated by the work of people like Carlo Scarpa, bringing sensitive modern architecture to their work with old buildings. During this time I learned skills that have underpinned the conservation elements of my practice ever since.

Which skill has been the most important for you in achieving success?

In the early years, I was always seeking opportunities for career moves and picking up work. Being prepared to work hard has always been important in my experience.

When I first started working with the small Italian practice, I was the first woman they had employed. They wanted me to work from home at first, because they thought it would be too distracting for the men for me to be working in the studio all the time. I was soon permanently based in the studio, but it shows you what attitudes were sometimes like at that time. Tenacity and self-belief are important to achieving success.

What has been the most significant lesson you have learned from a mistake or something that went wrong on a project?

Domestic clients are particularly challenging as from job to job they vary enormously. When doing work for people you know, it is important to explain to them right from the very first meeting that while you are their architect you have to put the 'friendship' to one side in order to give them the best professional service.

On one project a client who wanted to save money at every turn became more involved in her dealings with the contractor than was wise or in line with the JCT contract that was in place. When some difficult contractual issues arose she then wanted to hold her architect responsible. On the other hand, I once took on some work for an immediate neighbour, which obviously potentially brings particular challenges, and I had to be very clear that when I was wearing my architect's hat I needed to be professional and independent in the administration of the contract. Having set the ground rules, the project went very well.

Particularly when you are working in the domestic project sector, repeat work and referrals from past clients are critical to developing your business, so managing these relationships is a key concern.

What do you feel have been the hardest barriers to overcome in achieving your success, and how have you dealt with them?

Over my career I have worked in many different types and sizes of practice. I spent time in the public sector, working with the London Borough of Haringey and the London Borough of Camden, running complex estate action projects and operating in senior management roles. I have also worked in the culture of a large metropolitan practice at Allies and Morrison, and I now run my own practice as a sole practitioner.

I loved all the jobs I had in central London, but I hated commuting in the rush hour. When my daughter was born, my then employers had good maternity provision – six months on full pay followed by six months on half pay. However, the combination of long hours in the office and a long journey to and from work left little energy and time for life outside work. I hated not seeing my young daughter until the evening; the anxiety of the commute; worrying about being able to pay for the nanny. Deciding to establish my own practice and work from home was the best decision I ever made, as I was around every day when my daughter came home from school. Being based at home allows me to swim every morning and prepare nice food in my own kitchen, while still being able to put in 8 to 10 hours of work in a day. That decision did involve risks as well, but now I earn more money and have achieved a better work–life balance, and I enjoy the more direct client relationships and intensity of design process that come with running your own practice.

In identifying future leaders in your business, what characteristics and qualities do you look for?

Clearly leaders need talent, but also the ability to inspire others. I admired in Graham Morrison at Allies and Morrison his ability to make young architects believe that they could achieve the goals that he set them, as opposed to the more modest aims that they might have set for themselves. He was able to persuade young architects that they could stretch themselves.

At a time when there was still significant prejudice within the architecture profession, Graham recognised the huge contribution that women can make to architecture, and in return many talented women helped Allies and Morrison to achieve its success. The years I spent at Allies and Morrison were very influential in shaping my own career.

What are your goals in architecture, and have they changed over the course of your career?

I have enjoyed working in both the public and the private sectors of the profession and on large and small projects. Without the breadth of experience I gained before setting up my own practice I would have been less well prepared for what I do now. You need experience to provide you with credibility with clients. Although my current work is mainly domestic, I regularly take on projects up to half a million pounds in value, and clients need to know that you have the capability and capacity to deliver. The client needs to be confident that the architect has the skills necessary to undertake the project, so some track record is important. Experience enables you to be able to work more quickly and to understand the administrative systems that are so important to the efficient running of a practice. If you are running a small business then making effective and efficient use of your time is essential.

I am constantly focusing on new goals. Over the next few years I will be undertaking a project on my own house, including a basement construction. I will be embracing the challenge of BIM, launching a new practice website, striving to bring interesting and high-value projects into the practice and continuing to do some lecturing on Part 3 courses.

From your experiences, what do you think clients really want?

Clients need to feel that they can trust the architect to manage the project finances from inception through to completion. This means that you have to be comfortable talking about money from the outset. Make sure that you fully define the brief and understand how much budget is really available. Clients may be reluctant to reveal exactly what they wish to spend, preferring to keep some funds back, but making design changes later in the process is of course less cost effective, so it pays to try to achieve trust and transparency about the money. This includes being clear about your own fees. Many homeowner clients may have little knowledge about the construction process. You will need to explain the contractor's cash flow forecast and the role of a contingency.

Clients want the contractor to finish on time, so setting a realistic programme, monitoring progress and ensuring that the contractor has all the necessary information are crucial activities.

Clients need to feel that the completed project is what they wanted, and for their friends and family to tell them it's amazing!

From your experiences, what do you think contractors really want?

Contractors firstly want to make money, and there is nothing wrong with that.

Contractors want sufficient drawings and information to tell them what to do. Many architects fail to different degrees in this regard.

Smaller contractors also very much want to be appreciated. The choice of contractor is so important; it impacts fundamentally on the quality of work you will be able to achieve. I work with a relatively small pool of contractors and my working relationship with them is important to the success of my practice. Recognition and appreciation of what the contractor brings to the process is vital. Of course, contractors also want more work.

What do architects really want?

The next job
A good reputation
A portfolio of built work they can be proud of
A reasonable income
Mutual respect from contractors and the willingness to learn from each other

What is the main motivator that keeps you going?

It must be something in my blood. As I come into my office each day I have the feeling that there is so much to be done. It is also the feeling of excitement as a new building or space comes into being after months of imagining it in your head.

Who has been most influential in helping you to achieve your professional goals and ambitions?

The architect who came to our school and told us that being an architect was fun and that it was a career we could achieve was the person who set me off on my journey. The Italian Cultural Institute gave me a very generous scholarship, which enabled me to live, study and work in Florence, and this provided the initial catalyst for my professional life. Graham Morrison and Bob Allies helped me to believe in myself as an architect, to the point where they appointed me as their architect to do their own homes.

If you could add one thing to the architectural education curriculum, what would it be?

If I could add one thing it would be to spend a year working for a contractor on building sites: perhaps six months on an old building doing a refurbishment and six months on a new building.

What knowledge, skills and capabilities do you look for in newly qualified architects?

Newly qualified architects should be familiar with the work of a wide range of architects past and present. They need to be able to design in a way that is complementary to the designs produced by the office where they are applying for a job. A good knowledge of traditional and contemporary methods of construction is essential. For myself, I would ask, can you draw a sash window in plan and section? This is surprisingly difficult to do. Also, are you able to survey a small, but possibly complex building, and draw up the survey accurately? Can you research products to be specified and use National Building Specification? Younger architects often have the advantage that they can use all the current computer software.

Communication skills are also important: the ability to write an email or letter with the right professional tone and correct grammar; to be able to listen carefully and to liaise with clients or contractors over the phone and at meetings in a professional way.

What advice would you give to a newly qualified architect looking to make their way in the profession?

Always think of yourself as part of a team. That team will include clients, other professionals, contractors, sub-contractors and suppliers. Each one is important in producing a good building. Get as much experience as you can. Decide what kind of work you like and which architects inspire you and try to work for them. Be conscious of the opportunities within the practice as new jobs come in. There are benefits to broad experience, so consider moving to a few different offices, trying to get a more senior position with each move. It is good to remember from day one in your career the importance of contacts and connections – consultants, contractors, clients, suppliers – they can all be the sources of work in the future.

I would also say not to forget about the importance of achieving the right work–life balance for you. Measure your success in how you sleep at night and how good you feel each day as well as caring about your achievements and your bank balance.

What are the most important issues that will affect the business of architecture over the next decade?

The big increases in university tuition fees mean that the cost of architectural education is going to be an issue. I am not sure that the current position is sustainable.

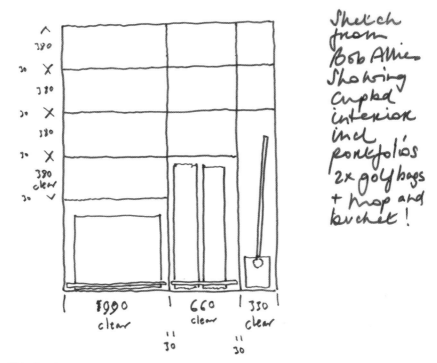

This sketch illustrates how detailed a client's brief can be, especially if the client is an architect. It shows a portfolio, two golf bags and a mop and bucket

I think we will see industry-wide use of BIM and also a lot of technological innovation in construction methods.

Government policy in relation to public procurement of buildings has a significant impact on architects, and it is becoming increasingly difficult for smaller practices to engage in public sector work. Whether this will change or not remains to be seen.

The cost of energy can only rise, and so energy efficiency of buildings will remain an important issue.

Architects will increasingly work for or with contractors. In fact, regardless of the particular procurement arrangements, we are always working in partnership with contractors.

The wider state of the UK economy is, of course, going to be a big factor for architects based in this country. In fact, a recession can sometimes be a good time for small practices. I generally find that in the boom times I have a lot of work in the suburbs and in a recession more of my work is in central London. Personally I have been busier than ever during the overall difficult economic times we have had since the banking crisis.

Would I do it again? Yes, it has been a wonderful and rewarding career.

06 BILL DUNSTER
ZEDfactory

Bill Dunster founded ZEDfactory in 1999. It has developed a highly respected track record for zero (fossil fuel) energy development (ZED) at a range of scales, from individual buildings, through larger-scale developments and eco-villages, to low carbon, low environmental impact urban master plans. One of ZEDfactory's largest single built developments is the Beddington Zero Energy Development (BedZED) housing scheme in the London suburb of Wallington, which in 2003 was the winner of the RIBA Sustainability Award and shortlisted for the RIBA Stirling Prize. As the first large-scale eco-community in the UK, BedZED has attracted considerable interest throughout the world for its approach to minimising ecological impact in both construction and operation.

Research and innovation is a central element of the success of ZEDfactory, and the practice has worked closely with the building products industry to develop new integrated renewable energy building elements. ZEDfactory has extended this expertise into other product development programmes outside the construction sector, including their ground-breaking solar electric ZEDbikes. The practice also works closely with academic researchers and consultants to model predicted energy consumption and production, fluid dynamics, daylighting and whole life cycle carbon costs of its designs to ensure that they achieve the lowest environmental impact possible. With Craig Simmons and Bobby Gilbert, Bill brought together the research that underpins his vision of a low carbon future in the ZEDbook,[3] which in 2008 received the RIBA President's Award for Outstanding Professional Practice-located Research.

Bill talks about how the breadth of opportunities offered by architecture to undertake work that is both creative and contributes to the building of a better society first fired up his enthusiasm for a career as an architect, and how grappling with the challenge of making climate neutral buildings the norm rather than the exception continues to keep him highly motivated today. He describes how ethics and values, driven by concerns about environmental degradation, climate change and over-dependence on depleting fossil fuel resources, are at the core of his practice and identity as an architect. In his interview, Bill provides us with a fascinating insight into the ZEDfactory approach to climate-led design, collaborative building product development and innovation in procurement and supply chain models, which challenge current construction industry conventional wisdom.

Why did you become an architect?
There was a beautiful apple orchard opposite the house where I grew up in suburban London. A property developer felled the orchard and built a load of neo-Georgian speculative homes. I just thought: 'There has to be a better way than this.' I guess I was motivated by

03__Bill Dunster, Craig Simmons and Bobby Gilbert, *The ZEDbook* (Abingdon, Oxon: Taylor and Francis, 2007).

anger and a feeling that I could do a better job. We do need to develop land and provide homes, but we need better models.

I am interested in the connection between different aspects of society, culture, technology. This is really what architecture is all about – joining up a diversity of human activities and trying to create an equitable future. If you can reconcile many different parameters and create something that offers optimism, beauty and a confidence that there can be a future that works, then that is something very positive and precious. If you don't think society is working properly, then architecture is an area in which you can operate and have an impact, and that was the appeal for me.

At the moment I don't think our society does work. We are depleting our natural resources and dangerously dependent on fossil fuels. To me there is not much point in individual self-advancement if the collective society is on a crash course to oblivion. I believe that if you feel you can make a plan for a future that is viable, you should do something about it. In a sense that is my personal professional code of conduct.

Designing energy-intensive buildings for multi-nationals might bring you wealth and peer endorsement. It might be fun, but it is not really in the collective interest. We need to look for a more enlightened self-interest. There is a consensus that environmental degradation is widespread and severe. The next generation is doing something about it. In our practice we just try to show alternative routes, philosophies and strategies, which can be beautiful and can contribute to solving these difficult problems. It doesn't matter if we don't always get it right, but it does matter that we are trying.

What has been the single most rewarding experience in your career so far?

When we had the 10th anniversary of the BedZED housing community, a kid who had been born and raised there gave an inspiring presentation about what it had meant to grow up there. It was fantastic to be able to hear that it's a good place to live and call home. We are clear that there are benefits to what we do, and that is the reward. You can look around the other housing estates near to BedZED and see that there is a huge difference. We try to quantify those differences and show developers what we can do. I hope that once they see the difference that can be made they won't opt for the current standard product.

Fundamentally, as a practice we think the current construction industry is pretty awful and that change is needed. Changing the procurement structures, innovating new products: we are focused on achieving this change. That is why we do lots of research and development work and engage closely with system and product developers. We are looking for the economies of scale to make our approach more widely applicable. Every year we are gaining ground, because everyone is being forced to deal with reduced resources, fossil fuel prices are escalating, opinion is changing. We now have projects where the building is generating more energy than it uses. We are not driven by design standards but by how buildings really perform. The aim is to reduce the carbon footprint of the structure, to maximise energy efficiency and to achieve the greatest possible level of on-site power generation. There is nothing especially new in this. Climate neutral buildings must be the aim and contributing to a secure future for human civilisation is the reward.

Which skill has been the most important for you in achieving success?

I would say determination, closely followed by ingenuity. You have to maintain a constant course, and not allow yourself to be knocked off your route by recession or politics. You need a plan that will work in the short term but that will also last you for decades. As a practice we have been trying to solve the same basic problems for more than 20 years, and you do get better at it. You gradually learn how to do things more efficiently at lower cost We have put a lot of determination and ingenuity into product development: improving solar panel materials, developing photo-voltaics that are integrated with roof and rain screen cladding. We are trying to change the rules of architecture, to show the construction and development industry the possibility of a different way of working. The benefits are colossal. We genuinely believe that a future of climate neutral buildings and cities is possible. It can also create a new aesthetic and a new urbanism. But we also need a new supply chain.

So we do have a very clear plan. I am hoping that gradually it will become clearer to clients and users that there are benefits to abandoning business as usual. That in turn will create a greater demand for this alternative approach and bring the necessary efficiencies of scale.

What has been the most significant lesson you have learned from a mistake or something that went wrong on a project?

I think my biggest mistake has been to be too optimistic. Perhaps over-ambition is nearly as problematic as apathy! You have to be realistic in setting your targets and goals. There is definitely a need to understand commercial constraints to the hilt. We use our projects to try to move things forward step by step, demonstrating single aspects of innovation. In this way we influence the development of aspirations, standards and regulations. We would certainly have made more money if we had always just done what we were told to do. Don't expect too many thanks and plaudits for trying to do the right thing. There are few prizes for good behaviour.

What do you feel have been the hardest barriers to overcome in achieving your success, and how have you dealt with them?

The biggest barrier to our progress has been British conservatism and social inertia. It isn't easy communicating that there is a serious environmental and resource problem; people want to believe that everything will be OK. Now we concentrate on promoting the solutions rather than pointing out the problems. All of these climate- and resource-related issues have been predictable, and the basic problem is now more widely recognised and the need for change somewhat more accepted. We do also make a lot of effort to make the commercial case for our approach.

In identifying future leaders in your business, what characteristics and qualities do you look for?

Most of our people come to us; they actively seek us out. We tend to have people in the practice who are self-motivated and want to do something, to contribute. They have to be robust and able to support an argument, and in our field of operation they need technical dexterity and expertise and to be able to work in the multi-disciplinary way that is so essential to our innovation strategy.

Quite a number of our staff members have come from other countries. Sometimes they return and set up their own practices along the lines of our model. There are now such practices in China, Brazil and the Netherlands.

What are your goals in architecture, and have they changed over the course of your career?

I am working to a long-term plan based on a core set of values. We do change emphasis within the practice from time to time. We now think that climate change is occurring to an even greater extent than we used to. I don't think we anticipated the full extent and impact of the increase in flooding we have experienced in the UK. So you can't completely predict the future; but many of the main trends are clear – the need to design for an ageing population demographic in western Europe, for example.

It surprises me that there isn't a more honest discussion in the architecture profession about the real challenges. As society becomes more short term in its horizons there is a real danger of long-term thinking being abandoned. In some ways China is actually looking more to the longer-term horizon, whereas the UK seems to lack vision.

From your experiences, what do you think clients really want?

Clients do need return on their investment, both short- and long-term. I think they also have a duty to make sure that they haven't damaged society. Development inevitably means change. A sophisticated client tries to understand the wider implications of their activities, but there are many that do not. There seems to be a lack of the concept of long-term commitment and making a contribution to the future. A professional architect must have a contract with the wider society. Part of the problem is that even within a professional body like the RIBA there is not agreement. Is architecture just a dilettante activity whose only responsibility is to art? Of course not, but equally neither is architecture only a form of engineering. That is the challenge. For our practice, we need to show clients the tangible benefits of a reduction in environmental impact.

From your experiences, what do you think contractors really want?

Contractors seek turnover; the money.

As a practice we now know the cost of every single component with which we work. In a way we are morphing into also being a contractor. We can now create a climate neutral home for the same sum as a Code 3 (UK Code for Sustainable Homes) house. The big challenge is to get rid of all the risk pricing. In our own procurement approach we have rethought the delivery model, the building components and the supply chain. You have to try an alternative to the traditional main contractor or developer model.

What do architects really want?

Architects want to express themselves in whatever way matters to them. The desire for creativity is very central. To be truthful, they are trying to impress their peers. That's what generates the energy for all those late-night working sessions in the schools of architecture, in the practices.

I don't think there is any substitute for working out for yourself what it is you are trying to do, not following someone else's approach. Do you want to be a follower or to set the rules? The same thing applies to things like energy and sustainability standards. People often want to just follow a standard because it is sitting there on a plate for them, but you need to think through carefully what is the right approach for each project.

What is the main motivator that keeps you going?

I couldn't sleep at night if I just stopped. I still want to find solutions to these big problems. There is no point in being rich but troubled. There is a connection between ethics and physical and mental wellbeing.

Who has been most influential in helping you to achieve your professional goals and ambitions?

We have certainly had plenty of exposure to lots of people we don't want to emulate.

If you could add one thing to the architectural education curriculum, what would it be?

I would simply ask that all students should produce a comprehensive statement of their ideas about how society should work 50 years from now. Architects should have a long-term vision and planning horizon, otherwise they are a liability to the society they serve.

What knowledge, skills and capabilities do you look for in newly qualified architects?

Whatever your skills and qualities, you need to complete your architectural education in the right practice context for you. I think the critical thing is to find the right place to do your apprenticeship, so I suppose we are looking for people who are in the right place with us.

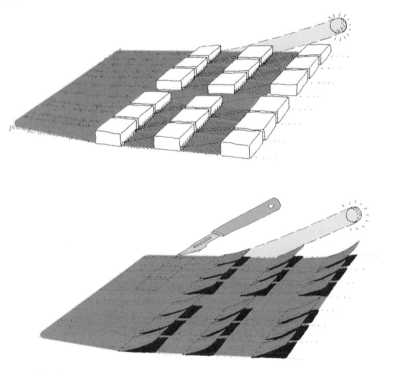

The new garden city

What advice would you give to a newly qualified architect looking to make their way in the profession?

Don't worry; architecture remains a viable profession. Nobody else is going to reconcile all these different conflicting parameters. We design the places for people to work, live, enjoy life – this enables civilisation to function.

What are the most important issues that will affect the business of architecture over the next decade?

There is always the threat that others will encroach upon the function of the architect. The role of the architect could become the role of the lifestyle engineer or some such thing. It is the substance of what is being done that is important.

You do need a diversity of people and inputs, different aspects and disciplines to create good buildings and cities. The architect adds value at the interfaces between the disciplines.

It is a great profession, because it is giving the direction of travel to society, but to be the best profession we need the right people, so attracting the very best to architecture is part of the future challenge.

CAROLINE BUCKINGHAM
HLM ARCHITECTS

As a shareholder and board director, Caroline Buckingham has a key strategic and communication role at HLM Architects and provides architectural and commercial leadership on large-scale projects and procurement frameworks in the UK and internationally. Caroline is also Head of Education Design for HLM. She acts as a client design adviser and regularly publishes articles and speaks at conferences on designing and procuring schools, colleges and university buildings. Among Caroline's current projects is the masterplanning of a new university in Abu Dhabi and an all-through learning school campus in Devon.

Caroline played an important part in negotiating a management buyout of HLM Architects from its US parent company in 2004, and has since been central to its subsequent growth and development. Her business leadership activities in recent years have seen her managing the acquisition of two other established and respected practices: Llewelyn Davies and Sidell Gibson.

A focus on the needs of end users and the use of effective communication skills are core elements of Caroline's approach to architecture. She also talks about the need to be able to maintain a strategic overview of projects and not become trapped in the detail. Caroline offers insights into the opportunities and barriers that you find in developing a career within an established practice, and identifies the mix of skills that practices need. She comments on some of the unique challenges of undertaking mergers and acquisitions in the field of architecture.

Why did you become an architect?

I didn't grow up thinking I wanted to be an architect from a young age, but I was always a maker and a builder as a child; tree houses and go-carts as I got older. At school I enjoyed art, and design and technology. In fact, I was the first girl at my school to do A level design and technology. My first idea was to go to art school, but my parents suggested studying architecture. Perhaps they thought it had more of a career focus. Nobody in my family was an architect. There were lots of teachers and people working in the arts, but there was no family tradition in architecture.

What has been the single most rewarding experience in your career so far?

I have spent a lot of time on schools projects. It is an area I find very rewarding, but it takes a lot of time and effort to deliver what the various stakeholders and the teachers and students really want. I had been working very hard. HLM attended the *Sunday Times* Small Companies Awards in 2009, and I had a big shock when they announced that I had won the award for best engagement with schools and colleges. I hadn't even been told that I had been nominated and I was thrilled to bits.

For me architecture is all about the end users. My interest is in social architecture and the user experience; it is not the iconic architecture approach.

Which skill has been the most important for you in achieving success?

I believe that I am a good listener, and that has been an important skill for me. Another attribute is that I don't allow myself to get bogged down in detail; I can take a strategic all-round view. Sometimes architects can struggle with the complexity of factors with which you have to deal, and take refuge in specific aspects. You also have to be able to engage and communicate, and this is something I am good at and enjoy. You can be an outstanding designer, but you also have to be able to get your message across. It is important to be able to talk with passion about your design without coming over as arrogant. That goes back to the need to balance talking with listening.

What has been the most significant lesson you have learned from a mistake or something that went wrong on a project?

All problems can be solved. It might seem terrible at the time, but it won't be the end of the world or even your career. You always need to stay focused on finding a solution. Don't be embarrassed about asking for support and advice because everyone makes mistakes.

When I was quite newly qualified I was working on a fairly standard office building that was going to be constructed on a steeply sloping site in Sheffield. It was a traditionally procured project and I was looking after the whole process including the construction administration. I really wanted to get everything right. When they did the setting out, one corner of the building was effectively off the corner of a cliff and the foundation designs had to be substantially changed. I think I got away with it at the time by a bit of allowance for youth, but I was prepared to own up straight away to my mistake. Everyone pulled together and found a structural solution at relatively little cost. You absolutely have to work together as a team in those types of situations.

Site levels must be my achilles heel, because I also remember a housing scheme in Milton Keynes where we had some of the slab levels incorrect. I went to site and was confronted with two swimming-pool-sized holes. You always have to front up to your errors if you have got things wrong. Architecture is all about problem-solving, and being nimble!

What do you feel have been the hardest barriers to overcome in achieving your success, and how have you dealt with them?

I have been through two major recessions. Construction is a volatile game. I have worked my way up through one practice. There can be barriers to progression if you follow that route: always hitting the glass ceiling of those above you and having to wait for opportunities to open up. Fortunately, I was able to participate in a management buyout and jump up to that more senior level. Career development routes in architecture are very ill-defined. Do you go it alone and set up a practice, or commit to an existing practice and try to move up the hierarchy?

In identifying future leaders in your business, what characteristics and qualities do you look for?

We look for people with a good mix of skills and try not to be too prescriptive. Generally the best leaders tend to be the all-rounders, but you do need some very strong designers. We try to build teams with complementary skills. Our associate directors work in pairs – almost like the advertising industry model. My advice would be to focus on what you are good at and you should progress.

What are your goals in architecture, and have they changed over the course of your career?

I have never consciously set out a career plan. I don't set myself specific personal goals to be achieved in a specific time frame. I live for the moment. It is important to me that I am enjoying what I am doing, that I feel passionate and switched on. In 2006 I saw that the education sector was growing and that this was an opportunity for HLM. Perhaps it was the teaching gene in me. So I really focused on promoting us in the education sector, and it paid off. It wasn't an area we had been very active in but it became 45% of our business. I do write business strategies and identify key positions. I enjoy the research element of business development: looking at current trends, analysing markets, evaluating funding arrangements.

Doing acquisitions has been very interesting. I don't take a particularly branded view of architecture, and so I have been able to work well with other cultures and people in bringing different practices together. I like sharing knowledge, learning new things and avoiding complacency. Architecture attracts some strong personalities. This can make mergers between practices quite challenging, and many don't succeed. With our acquisitions we have left the businesses with their own brands and cultures. I hope that I bring new business skills to these practices. It is an area that I think we are generally weak in as a profession.

From your experiences, what do you think clients really want?

Clients want flair and imagination, but delivered in a clear, concise and understandable way. They generally initially choose your practice for your culture and design approach. They see your work and want to meet with you and see if you can understand each other. They want us to deliver a shared vision, but they need clarity about what it will cost and how long it will take. These are fundamentals in every project that cannot be avoided.

Sometimes clients seem quite surprised by what emerges from the ground on site, even when you have produced extensive drawings, models and visualisations. You have to think carefully about what you need to give to clients to explain the scheme and enable them to understand what they are getting, particularly with smaller clients. An experienced and seasoned client will know what they are looking for, but those with less prior experience of the design and construction process will need more time and support. You do become a bit of a confidant. Sometimes you have to deal with quite emotional aspects while maintaining a professional working relationship.

From your experiences, what do you think contractors really want?

They definitely want to make a bob or two, but a good contractor is usually also very proud of their quality and workmanship. We recently hosted an internal conference with our teams and we invited some contractor clients. Everyone was asked to pick out their best projects that we had done together. One of the contractors picked a scheme that we probably wouldn't have considered one of our best, but it made the best profit margin for them. So there are very different drivers. In the end, I don't think many architects are primarily motivated by money.

If it is contractor-led procurement, you still need to meet end-user needs, and achieving that is quite an art. You have to manage expectations on all sides and focus on maintaining quality. Contractors are taking a more prominent role generally and employing design managers. I think that can cause continuity to be lost.

What do architects really want?

We just want to draw, talk about design and experience architecture. Most architects don't really want to deal with all the bureaucracy and paperwork that comes with the territory nowadays. Architects do enjoy the people side of things, I think. They never know when to stop designing, which can impact on profitability. For architects, design is a never-ending process.

What is the main motivator that keeps you going?

Interacting with really interesting people is probably my main motivator. The new challenges that each new project brings keeps things fresh. Every client is different, every project is different; new locations and new types of buildings. You do need occasional time out, though. As a profession we should be encouraging travel and sabbaticals – you come back a better and wiser person.

Who has been most influential in helping you to achieve your professional goals and ambitions?

At school it was my design and technology teacher. The careers teacher had told me that 'girls don't do architecture'. My design and technology teacher was outraged and told me that I would do well in architecture if I enjoyed it.

I have enjoyed a great support network of family, friends and work colleagues.

I also love listening to good speakers – business leaders. At first I wasn't very good at public speaking, but you do need to develop skills and confidence in presentation. I go to events at the Institute of Directors, where you can hear a fantastic range of people. Some are even better than you might expect and others are not as strong as you have anticipated, but you always learn something. I also go to the Institute of Directors' annual Women as Leaders conference.

If you could add one thing to the architectural education curriculum, what would it be?

I believe that there should be a stronger connection between practice and education. Training should be more blended with practice, with greater contact between practitioners and academics. I think that students would benefit from a better understanding of real-world problems.

It is now a globalised profession, but schools of architecture can become inward-looking. The good schools bring in external views and personalities.

What knowledge, skills and capabilities do you look for in newly qualified architects?

As a starting point they need to have a good, competent design portfolio. Then for me it is all about enthusiasm and passion. Will they come into the practice with energy and make a mark? Recent years have been tough economically, and having the energy of younger architects in the practice with their knowledge and enthusiasm for new technologies and new approaches has been important in keeping us all motivated. The older folks have things to teach the young ones, but the youngsters also have a great deal to teach us.

What advice would you give to a newly qualified architect looking to make their way in the profession?

Be confident, but not arrogant. Get as much and as varied experience as you possibly can. Try different practices with different cultures. When you go for interviews, ask about the work the practice does and how it operates. Don't be too pushy, but show that you are genuinely interested. You'll soon begin to work out your natural career path in what is a very diverse profession. Identify your strengths and weaknesses and decide which facets of architecture really appeal. If you can find a niche that interests you – say, passive energy design or healthcare design – and become expert in it, then that can set you apart from your peers. Alternatively, you might decide that you don't want to follow the traditional architectural career path. There are many other roles that architects are very suitable for. I would say don't be afraid to put yourself forward for other roles. Don't be boxed in by a narrow definition of the architecture profession.

What are the most important issues that will affect the business of architecture over the next decade?

There is a real risk of the dilution and diminution of the profession through incursion and competition from others. This isn't always a good thing in terms of the interests of clients and end users, but we will need to be able to justify our place in the process and our influence. The architecture profession will need to adapt and change, and we will need views from younger generations to influence how our professional institutions develop.

I think that there will be intense competition from other countries. British architecture has a great reputation internationally, but we will need to work hard to maintain that position. We can't be complacent. All industries have to be acutely aware of both threats and opportunities. We can't afford to be old-fashioned in our outlook or trapped by tradition.

Lots of people want to become architects; it remains a very popular university course, so there must be something attractive about the profession. We absolutely must use this to our advantage, to attract the very best young people and to strengthen the profession.

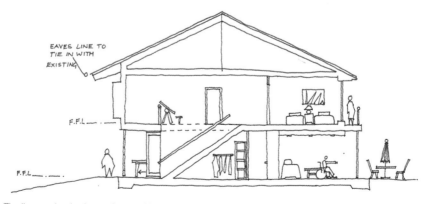

The live, work, play house for watching the world go by

08 TIM BAILEY
XSITE ARCHITECTURE

Architecture is increasingly an international commodity, with practices tending to cluster in key metropolitan centres such as London, New York and Hong Kong. However, while the practice of architecture is inevitably subject to the forces of globalisation, there are some architects who recognise and promote the relevancy of a more local context.

Born in the north-east of England, Tim Bailey made a positive decision to stay in the region after graduating from Newcastle University and went on to create a practice with both a strong and distinctive design ethos and a commitment to engagement with its local context and communities. In particular, xsite architecture has developed a reputation for collaborative working with the arts sector and for arts clients, as well as working in the retail, leisure, residential and commercial sectors.

Tim explains what drives his own ambitions in pursuing the art and profession of architecture and how, despite the initial challenges, establishing his own practice has enabled him to achieve success on his own terms.

Why did you become an architect?
I was fascinated from an early age by materials, dimensions and how things are assembled to make objects. However, my first career ambition was to join the Navy, to which my dad said 'No!' At some point I discovered that a man who lived across the road was the Hartlepool Borough Architect. My father was a journalist and my mother a teacher, so architecture was outside the family experience, but I became curious as to what the job of an architect might be about and what it might mean you could do. At around the age of 16, I discussed this with a careers teacher, but the only information that could be found was a little leaflet on 'Being an architect in the NHS'.

At university I began to understand that architecture is really a social science with an artistic basis, and that is still how I view the practice of architecture. I have never questioned what else I might do, so it must suit me.

What has been the single most rewarding experience in your career so far?
Completing the Boho 1 project in Middlesbrough was both a very rewarding experience and an important milestone for my practice, xsite architecture. This workspace project for digital start-up companies was a breakthrough project when the practice was five years old, and a significant regeneration project for the town, helping to incubate new businesses and create a cluster of enterprise activity. At that time the University of Teesside was beginning to establish a reputation in digital visualisation technologies and Middlesbrough was keen to hold on to the talent being developed. Making a real impact on the lives of communities is very important to me.

Which skill has been the most important for you in achieving success?

I would say that the key skills for me have been an ability to get the early thinking right, to persist with an iterative approach to the design process, and to work out what are the best creative, sustainable solutions for each project, rather than repeating previous models and solutions. This has marked the practice out. Not too many people put a high value on thinking and thinking time, but clients really are interested in the outcomes from that type of intense and deep thought process.

When we were completing Boho 1 it was found that one of the floor spaces could not be rented out in its entirety, and we were asked if we could offer a solution to sub-divide the space, but with the option to return to a single floor plate and occupancy if the economic situation changed in the future. We built four micro office spaces using standard pallets and our own labour at a cost of just £7,000. They looked funky and suited the context. We know our limitations, but in this case the lateral thinking and willingness to get stuck in paid off. We still do some of our own making and assembly for exhibitions and temporary installations. The practice gets the labour costs as well as the design fee, and we enjoy doing it. In the end the aggregate rent for the four micro office spaces turned out to be better than the single floor plate rentals.

We try not to relate our fees directly to the construction cost. We now have a reputation for coming up with different answers, and we want our fees to reflect the value we add in this way.

What has been the most significant lesson you have learned from a mistake or something that went wrong on a project?

There is always a danger with my approach of getting over-involved; being too willing to do anything to make things happen. I once did the setting out on site of the foundations for a project myself, and as I was doing it I remember thinking, 'What if I get this wrong?' It is important not to overreach the limits of your competence and role, at least most of the time! It's also vital not to over-promise and then not deliver.

What do you feel have been the hardest barriers to overcome in achieving your success, and how have you dealt with them?

I worked for 10 years in a practice that focused mainly on the housing sector, working my way up to partnership in a 50-strong practice. However, in the end I wasn't working to my own agenda. In setting up my practice I made a conscious decision that I wanted to work on more cultural projects, and so I haven't chased work in other sectors. Neither have I chased growth for its own sake. In building a successful practice you've got to stay true to your core values.

The biggest barrier to establishing a practice in the early years is establishing credibility; persuading people that you can do it. For me the trick was to establish small targets and take it step by step. I set realistic goals and showed that I had delivered. I did a lot of networking in the local and regional arts community, and of course you also need a bit of luck.

Personally, I am very committed to my locality. The geography – cultural, physical, and economic – of the North East is central to what we do. It might be possible to get established more quickly by moving to one of the bigger centres, but that isn't what we are about. That said, it means it is even more important that we take our opportunities when we can. Now we are seen as a strong regional voice. Out of about 30 or so local authorities in the North East, we have worked, or are working, with about half. It is about context, scale and culture, and it needs to run through the collective veins of the practice. Part of the credibility comes from the fact that if you are based there you have to live with the consequences of your decisions and actions. You can't fly in and out. It leaves you exposed socially as well as technically and professionally, which can be scary.

In identifying future leaders in your business, what characteristics and qualities do you look for?

I am looking for people who are smart and committed, who have talent but also street intelligence. It is always interesting to see how individuals wear their talent. You need to find people who understand their own skills and how best to utilise them. Future leaders will emerge from those architects in their mid-20s to mid-30s who take an interest in the broader factors. They have to be able to network, to understand the core values of the business, and in our practice to understand the urban geography and history of the places in which we work. The need to demonstrate credibility and a desire to have an impact are deeply embedded in those we are looking for, not just an ambition to move up a level in the career hierarchy.

What are your goals in architecture, and have they changed over the course of your career?

My fundamental goals haven't changed at all. I want to do work that impacts positively upon communities, whether that is through buildings, landscape or even demolition. My view of architecture as a social science and artistic endeavour is the core driver of my practice.

From your experiences, what do you think clients really want?

Clarity, insight and foresight. If you can show your clients that you can help them to realise their dream then they will rarely pull the rug. They do expect the architect to understand costs and cost management, though. In the end, it is all about good communication.

From your experiences, what do you think contractors really want?

Essentially, contractors want the same as clients, but they don't want to lose money. Integrity and trust are very important in all these relationships.

What do architects really want?

Architects need and want happy clients and contractors. Of course we also want to be taken seriously, but in order to get that we need to deliver what is required; then you will get the recognition. The artistic vision alone is not enough, unless you are one of the 0.001% of signature architects, and even they got to that position by delivering on their promises. Thinking that you will get there on your artistic vision alone is a recipe for disappointment. But delivering what you promised is rewarding.

What is the main motivator that keeps you going?

For me nothing else would be as rewarding or interesting as practising architecture. At the time when we were struggling to win bigger projects, a couple of in-house posts came up with Newcastle City Council in areas of culture and regeneration that were really of interest to me, matched my skills well, and offered the opportunity to have a very real and lasting impact, and I was tempted to have a go. In the end I wasn't sure if the inevitable politics, paperwork and endless meetings would have left sufficient room for actual creativity. It would have been more the role of producer than of director. I can best make a difference as an architect.

Who has been most influential in helping you to achieve your professional goals and ambitions?

There have been three people who have influenced me a great deal. The first was David Banks, who was one of the partners in the first office I worked in. David was a technical guru who knew the Building Regulations inside out and who approached everything from playing the guitar to practising architecture with a mathematician's precision. Although my design approach is very different, I learned from David the crucial importance of being well read and well researched in your areas of expertise, and the sense of confidence that comes from knowing that your opinions and strategies are underpinned by thorough knowledge.

John Noddings was another former work colleague who taught me key lessons. He was rooted in the local, and was passionate about the North East and the work he did there. It is the importance of a passionately held set of values and beliefs related to what you do that John gave to me.

My third influential figure was Cyril Winskell, who was for many years a conservation architect at Newcastle City Council. I think of Cyril as the wily old dog of the parish, who understood the system and how to apply knowledge and authority to make things happen. He also showed me the importance of staying power.

David, John and Cyril weren't really mentors or formal collaborators but they all influenced my approach to trying to have real impact.

If you could add one thing to the architectural education curriculum, what would it be?

My answer would be 'Funky Business: why numbers matter'. I wouldn't try to bring business skills in that MBA sense into the curriculum, but there is a real need for graduates to have some understanding of the basic principles of income, expenditure, time and fees that underpin a successful practice. In the end there has to be a profit motivation if a practice is to survive and thrive, and a comprehension of some basic business skills can be applied in many ways. Financial resources can used in different ways and you can be creative and inventive in your approach to the use of money and other resources in your practice. It would be good if students could be shown examples of how successful creative businesses can be run, so that they can understand the business context they are entering. Marketing is also a proper area of study that should be addressed. You need to be able to promote yourself in the job market and be able to think creatively about how you can help your practice to communicate its services.

What knowledge, skills and capabilities do you look for in newly qualified architects?

I would sum this up in one word – aptitude. As an architect you have got to be able to design, to speak convincingly and to take instructions. When employing newly qualified architects we don't assume a deep level of specific practice-related knowledge, but we do require diligence, an inquiring mind, the ability to assimilate and utilise knowledge and information, and a desire to communicate. Drawing remains core to how architects communicate, so highly developed drawing skills are an essential.

What advice would you give to a newly qualified architect looking to make their way in the profession?

Look out for opportunities. Help your immediate boss as much as possible; become indispensable to them. Become an expert in something useful to the practice. Work quickly where possible, but don't neglect thinking time. As you move further into your career, your practice will be keen to see if you have got the aptitude and attitude to turn opportunities into real activity. Keep an eye out for possible sites and new clients – these will always be of interest to your practice.

What are the most important issues that will affect the business of architecture over the next decade?

It will become increasingly difficult to make the growth leaps in business size from small to medium and medium to large practice. Client attitudes to risk and liability and procurement approaches are making this harder. In many ways, I think that as a profession we have been too willing to accept too much liability; we need to think more about mechanisms such as financial caps on liability and more carefully defining the scope of our services. Part of the solution may come through more collaborative working, whether with other architects and consultants or with contractors.

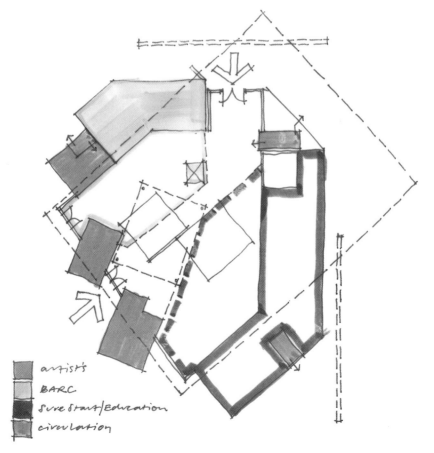

artist's
BARC
Sure Start/Education
circulation

Spatial planning diagram for flexibility of uses at Bolam Coyne, Byker Wall, Newcastle upon Tyne, 2004

Evolving technologies are also going to bring big changes. At the moment BIM is in quite an expansive and also expensive phase; it is becoming adopted quite quickly. Having said that, in 10 years' time we may be looking back at BIM as a 'has-been' technology. There is clearly going to be much more automation of the design and construction processes. The big data concept is beginning to gain momentum as well, but nobody yet seems to know how it will really work.

Sustainabilty will continue to be an important theme, with issues such as flood resilience coming to the fore.

In many ways the architecture profession is becoming more global, especially for the London-based practices. However, I am more interested in the local model. Some years ago I visited the practice of Gunter Behnisch, near Stuttgart, and was struck by his highly successful model of an innovative practice that is very much influenced by its specific location. I think there is space for an alternative to the homogenised global model.

09 SATWINDER SAMRA
SCHOOL OF ARCHITECTURE, UNIVERSITY OF SHEFFIELD

An architect and educator, Satwinder Samra's architectural career began at innovative developers and urban regenerators Urban Splash, where he worked on several award-winning projects in Manchester and Liverpool. He later moved to Proctor and Matthews Architects to focus on social housing. In 1998 he returned north, founding Sauce Architecture with Daniel Jary in Sheffield. Their projects included the Chesterfield City Centre master plan with URBED and Arup, and new office headquarters for Balfour Beatty.

Currently, Satwinder is Director of Future Practice and Senior University Teacher at the University of Sheffield School of Architecture. Satwinder has lectured, reviewed and examined at a number of schools of architecture, including Glasgow School of Art, Bergen School of Architecture, Norway, and the Harbin Institute of Technology in China, and he was a judge for the RIBA President's Medals 2013.

Satwinder explains how a concern for user needs and architecture with a social purpose are central values that inform his approach to both architectural practice and education. He identifies the communication skills that are vital to achieving success in practice, encompassing the ability to listen and understand the requirements of clients, users and contractors, and the capability to persuade stakeholders of the possibilities and opportunities that architectural design can offer. For Satwinder, freehand drawing skills remain an important tool for architects to communicate and explore ideas. Satwinder is convinced of the need for the profession to demonstrate the social and culture value of architecture, but also speaks candidly about the lack of business acumen that can hinder some architects.

With insights from his own experiences of developing a career in architecture, Satwinder shares his concerns about the future diversity of the UK architecture profession in the context of a long programme of study and ever increasing university tuition fees. He describes some of his ideas for innovation in study routes and collaboration between architecture practices and students, to create better links between academia and industry.

Why did you become an architect?
From a very young age I was fascinated with drawing and making things. I remember taking home something I had made enthusiastically out of cereal boxes and paper at nursery and my mum being very proud of it. Even today she recounts this as early evidence of my architectural leaning!

I had an excellent secondary education and very supportive and encouraging parents. Design, technology and graphic communication was taught very well and I really enjoyed it. At around the age of 17, I considered studying aeronautical or civil engineering, but in the end I fixed on architecture. I think the appeal of architecture was that it seemed to offer the opportunity to make things better for people, and that social purpose is important to me.

I think we need to place more value on design; it's just as important as philosophy, politics and economics to the future prosperity, quality of life and happiness of the nation. Design and making is often dismissed as not being an academic activity and is marginalised in mainstream secondary education. I sense that kids often lose confidence in their creative skills in their teenage years.

There's lots of pressure on young people, from their parents, from the media, to weigh up university course fees against the likely future earnings in different careers. Clearly, there's a very real financial gap when it comes to architecture. Most student architects in the UK will never repay their loans and debts under the current fee regime. I fear that we are losing a generation of talented people. There is a real danger that financial barriers to architectural education will make the profession more elitist in its demographics. One possible solution that I am exploring might be for architecture schools to have closer links with practices on the development of collaborative and 'earn-as-you-learn' type models.

What has been the single most rewarding experience in your career so far?

Being part of a young, unknown team of designers, contractors and developers when I joined Urban Splash in 1994 was a very exciting and uplifting time for me. I was a project architect doing in-house design work, but I was also deeply involved in all aspects of the development process. We undertook an incredibly wide range of activities: designing apartment layouts, showing prospective buyers around empty warehouses and purchasing kitchen units. It was fascinating to see the things you were working on being realised very quickly. Because we were small and new, there was no fear. Perhaps it was just the naivety of youth, but we weren't overwhelmed by the bureaucracies of risk and compliance. There was also a real team ethos; there weren't the usual contractual fracture lines that often exist in the construction industry.

As an educator, I am always tremendously rewarded when students start to gain the confidence that they can really achieve things. We all question the value and merits of our work, but you need to embrace and overcome that area of doubt. I call it the positive grey. When students you have worked with start to get established in their careers – managing projects, winning awards, establishing practices – that is very satisfying.

Which skill has been the most important for you in achieving success?

I think that one very important attribute is having empathy for the people you are working for and with: clients, contractors, building users, researchers and students. You need to be able to tune in to other people's frequencies as quickly as possible, and that means listening as well as talking on the right wavelength.

The ability to draw fluently freehand has been very useful to me, as a tool for communication. I was fortunate to train at a time when you didn't need a laptop to mediate every design move. There is still a place for a live conversation between people using a pencil and a stack of paper. It can take place at any stage in a project.

What has been the most significant lesson you have learned from a mistake or something that went wrong on a project?

In my early career I once drew a section line the wrong way round on a drawing, resulting in a canopy being fabricated back to front. We managed to resolve it quite simply in the end. I remember the site agent saying to me, 'Don't worry; it's only a real blunder if it can't be sorted out.' It was a hard way to learn, though. It taught me that you always have to be diligent and conscientious in all that you do; you can't be casual. When you have a problem, you need to share it and seek support. It probably won't be as bad as you think, but you mustn't sit on it. I think it is important to clarify and manage expectations about what you are doing right from the start of a project. That helps you to build trust with the people you are working with.

What do you feel have been the hardest barriers to overcome in achieving your success, and how have you dealt with them?

It is still quite unusual for someone from a working-class, ethnic-minority background to enter the architecture profession. I haven't let that stand in my way. I have tried to let my work speak for itself and strived to do the very best that I can working with those around me. However, I doubt that I would be joining the profession today, given the funding issues around architectural education. I think as a 17-year-old now the prospect of the large debts built up over a long professional education process would worry me and act as a barrier. Family background and wealth do affect how people perceive financial risk. My own background gives me an insight into this. The profession could become even more exclusive, which would not be a good thing.

It can be frustrating dealing with people saying something is just not possible – often out of a kind of apathy or disproportionate risk aversion. You need to have the ability to draw and talk persuasively, to explain the real possibilities. Spreadsheets with numbers might give financial reassurance, but you need to be able to explain and analyse problems in other ways as well.

Universities need to consider how they can develop and nurture talented educators who may not be on a conventional academic career path. The issue around career development is currently being addressed and explored in my institution. As always, I am sure that Sheffield will lead the way on this. I was fortunate to win a Sheffield University Senate Award, which acknowledged my teaching work. There is still work to do in institutions to ensure that the importance of rigorous and dedicated teaching is maintained. Only then can we ensure that the next generation of architects are able to deal with the challenges they will face. There is potentially a rich interplay between research, education and practice, and it is important that we avoid the creation of silos.

In identifying future leaders in your business, what characteristics and qualities do you look for?

I would say patience, emotional intelligence, the ability to listen and the capacity to stay calm under pressure. These qualities can help a good architect to become an effective leader and a great architect.

Leaders in both practice and academia need to be able to speak about opportunities rather than problems. They have to be able to support, engage and excite those around them: staff, co-professionals, clients, contractors and students.

What are your goals in architecture, and have they changed over the course of your career?

I aim to produce work of merit that is socially inclusive. It could be a student brief, a seminar on communication, a client proposal, a feasibility study or a building project – whatever the activity, these basic values and aspirations are important to me. I do want to make a difference, to go beyond the simple provision of a service or building.

Over time I think I have become more user-focused and more conscious of things like the ageing demographic. I am less concerned about receiving the accolades of other architects, although that is an intrinsic part of our DNA. We do want the approval of our peers. It shouldn't be the main driver, but there is no doubt that professional credibility leads to new opportunities. However, it is a double-edged sword.

I have also become more interested in exploring what is the most you can achieve for the least amount of money – the careful use of limited resources – and less obsessed with shadow gaps.

From your experiences, what do you think clients really want?

Clients want to be heard, included, respected and amazed. It might not be the 'wow' factor as such, but clients do want something unique, insightful and with impact from their architect. Architects have great skills in research, analysis and visualisation, which as a profession we often underplay.

Good clients don't materialise by magic overnight; you have to build trust and develop relationships. Clients should expect a professional, rigorous and supportive service.

From your experiences, what do you think contractors really want?

A good contractor wants to build on time, to produce work of quality of which they can be proud, to be a part of the team and, of course, to make a profit. Working with Urban Splash taught me that contractors like it when you ask them questions. They have a lot of tacit knowledge that we often don't tap into.

I think the really big challenge is for us to rebuild the relationships between the designers and the real makers, to which there are many barriers in modern procurement methods.

What do architects really want?

Historically architects have wanted recognition, awards and to be held in esteem by their peers. This is changing. I think that there is a movement with younger architects towards wanting to fulfil a clear social purpose.

Architects do want to be paid appropriately, but we don't generally take this element seriously enough in the management of our businesses, in my opinion. We are quick to complain about levels of fees and remuneration, but seem unwilling to do very much about it.

What is the main motivator that keeps you going?

Knowing that you can make a difference is a key motivator. I remain inquisitive about people and the environment and how the two interact. Developing the confidence of students and helping them to find opportunities to start and develop their careers is central to my current motivation. I am also excited about the possibility of working with others to develop a better, more integrated relationship between the university schools of architecture and architectural practices.

Who has been most influential in helping you to achieve your professional goals and ambitions?

I am grateful to those people who have given me the space to get on with the job while offering support when needed. In the early years it was Jonathan Falkingham and Tom Bloxham at Urban Splash and their entrepreneurial, can-do approach that enthused and encouraged me. I found it very liberating. Jeremy Till, with whom I worked for a decade, has been an inspiration to me as an architect and educator. He combines wit and humour with a phenomenal intellect.

On a less personal level I am a great admirer of the work of Carlo Scarpa, not only for his creative output and tactile working methods but also for his ability to work directly with skilled contractors.

If you could add one thing to the architectural education curriculum, what would it be?

The thing I would like to see is more discussion of the relationships between economics, procurement and design. I believe we are already doing this at the University of Sheffield, and much of our best student design work emerges from schemes that are creatively influenced by these parameters.

What knowledge, skills and capabilities do you look for in newly qualified architects?

The ability to communicate is important, to be able to truly listen and to ask the right questions. They need a holistic approach to design, to be able to understand the complexities. Being able to draw and communicate through visual media is a must-have.

What advice would you give to a newly qualified architect looking to make their way in the profession?

They probably do need to be just a little bit canny, perhaps even a little bit opportunistic, but must ensure that they develop and demonstrate strong personal ethics and values. I would say seek out mentors. People like to be asked for advice. I would also encourage young professionals not to undersell themselves. Don't work for nothing.

What are the most important issues that will affect the business of architecture over the next decade?

I think that we will see a rise in the self-initiated project, where building users can work directly with digital technologies; the idea of file-to-factory. There is a real role for the architect as enabler in this, and it will potentially radically restructure the construction supply chain.

Environmental sustainability and the associated ethical stance of the architect is going to remain a major issue. Architects will need to think deeply about where they are placed in the context of that debate. Depleting fossil fuel energy supplies, climate change, ageing populations, restrictions in housing supply – these are major challenges facing society. Architects should place themselves at the centre of the debate, not be left sitting at the edges.

Another issue that I feel will be important is the whole matter of demonstrating the value of architecture. We can't just be a provider of services; we don't want the cultural and social value of what architects do to be lost and for our work to only be about systematic production.

You can clearly see an emerging bias towards the funding of science, engineering and technology-focused subjects, partly as a result of government policy and partly as a result of the new market forces in higher education. The supply of architecture students will change as fee levels increase; many will be nervous about embarking on an architectural course. If we are to continue to attract the very best to the profession we will need to think seriously about access and support for students from diverse backgrounds.

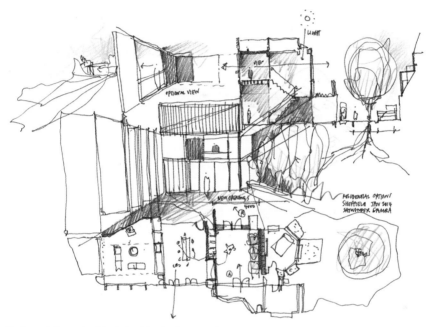

Study exploring potential relationships for 'House in Sheffield' Freehand sketch incorporating plan, section and perspective views

DAVID PARTRIDGE
ARGENT

After starting his professional life in conventional architectural practice, David Partridge switched sides in 1990, going from poacher to gamekeeper when he joined developer Argent, which delivers major mixed-use developments in many of the United Kingdom's major cities.

Appointed joint Chief Executive in 2006 and Managing Partner of the new Argent LLP in 2012, he oversees the master planning, design, financing and legal aspects of Argent's impressive portfolio of projects. This currently includes the hugely significant King's Cross urban regeneration project in London, in which a whole new city quarter is now rapidly emerging, including the creative re-use of 20 historic buildings and structures; and the innovative Airport City project at Manchester, which will see the creation of an enterprise zone in a setting of urban spaces and parkland.

David describes his journey from being an architect to becoming the client that architects now aspire to work with, the unique approach to development management that his in-depth understanding of the design process has inspired, and the skills he seeks and admires in the best architects. He also offers one or two friendly pointers as to how architects and the architectural profession might be able to up their game.

Why did you become an architect?
I have always wanted to be an architect, in fact from so far back that I can't really remember what first sparked my interest. At school, we did some psychometric tests before starting A levels that were supposed to show what careers we were most suitable for, and architect came top of my list. My teachers wondered how I had managed to fix the results.

It is the combination of art and science, the creative and pragmatic, that appeals to me. Of course there are a whole range of different types of people who work in architecture. Some are very creative, sometimes perhaps too creative, while others can be too dull and pragmatic, but the best architects get that blend of the artistic and the scientific approach just right. The thing that attracts me to architecture is that prospect of being able to soar with the eagles in terms of creating something wonderful while at the same time making the thing work and stand up. It's that classic quote – firmness, commodity and delight.

Why did you switch to being a developer?
My wife always says that I have the square hands of an engineer, not the long thin hands of an artist. I think I came to the gradual realisation that I am more into the 'fixing it' side rather than pure design. I know that I can't compete with the likes of Will Alsop. I felt that I could be creative in making the opportunities for others.

When I was a partner in architectural practice in the 1980s we had interesting work, mainly concentrated in the golden technology triangle in the M3–M4 corridor. I came to feel, though, that I wanted to move up the food chain, as I had become frustrated with bidding for projects that didn't come off and being so reliant on the decision-making of others. I was also struggling to find the right architectural language to express myself as an architectural practitioner. My interest and tastes in architecture are very eclectic and varied, and I hadn't found the architectural idiom or philosophy for which I could pin myself to the mast. So in 1989 I moved to Argent as a project and design manager and here I am now, running the new partnership. I am driven by the same thing at Argent as I was as an architect: the desire to make things happen and get things built.

What has been the single most rewarding experience in your career so far?

This is it. We are sitting in our offices in King's Cross at the heart of an area where we are bringing about a massive transformation of a significant part of one of the world's great cities. It is work at a scale far beyond that which I could effect as an architect in practice. The Argent offices in Manchester and Birmingham are similarly located within central city districts where we were able to facilitate major urban regeneration with huge impact. I get a tremendous buzz visiting those places and seeing what we have achieved; seeing people living, working and playing in these fantastic urban environments.

I once took a flight from Birmingham airport, and as we passed over the city I looked down and saw Brindleyplace from the air … what an experience to see a real city quarter from the air as a built reality, looking just like the initial master plan sketches, then the models and digital visualisations. Changing the world, making it a better place – I believe that is what most architects really want to do. For it to be a visible change is a great reward.

Which skill has been the most important for you in achieving success?

Both as an architect and as a developer, I would say that it has been my design training and skills and my understanding of the design process – all the things that need to be achieved to work through from the brief to the delivery – that have been central to achieving success.

Getting the brief right is so important. What are the artistic, financial, visionary and pragmatic factors that need to be addressed? It is this design focus and our brief-making skills that have given Argent a unique advantage. I can juggle the tax, finance, legal and regulatory stuff. In fact sometimes the elegant solution to unlocking a brief may be a legal agreement that balances the needs of different stakeholders, so creativity can take many forms. That understanding of the design process is the key asset, though. An accountant, an engineer, a lawyer, they would come from a different viewpoint. When you look around at the big developers you can tell which sort of professional backgrounds have got their hands on the tiller. At Argent we have people from all of those backgrounds, so we bring all of those skills to bear on any project,

Do architects think differently?

I think that architects always seek a solution that focuses on the highest common factor rather than the lowest common denominator. Engineers will sometimes only ask 'Will it work?' An architect will often ask 'How can I use this as a way to solve other problems as well?' Sometimes, of course, architects can have a tendency to lose sight of the basics, so they shouldn't allow themselves to be pulled along solely by the artistry, but there are some unique skills that come from architectural education.

What has been the most significant lesson you have learned from a mistake or something that went wrong on a project?

I feel most regret about some schemes where we perhaps trusted things just a bit too much to others and inadvertently gave up control. Sometimes this has happened when a plot has been sold to a builder/developer, and even within a strong urban design framework some of the artistry has been lost. You do need an element of 'control freakery' to achieve real quality – take Haussmann's Paris, for example.

What do you feel have been the hardest barriers to overcome in achieving your success, and how have you dealt with them?

Major development is a slow process, so you need deep reserves of patience and perseverance. There are layers and layers of complexity to work through, but at the same time you often need a simple core message for people to work with. The barriers to success are this complexity, which is made even more intricate because of the sheer numbers of people that are involved. Somehow in working through all this you have to keep hold of and keep articulating the fundamental vision. You have to be able to align people's aspirations. Sometimes this means asking people to give away things, but for mutual benefit rather than mutual dis-benefit. The main thing is to avoid the vision suffering a death by a thousand cuts.

In identifying future leaders in your business, what characteristics and qualities do you look for?

We take the business of enabling our staff to be successful within Argent very seriously. We have evolved a Skills and Abilities framework, which is used in our staff performance and development reviews. The aim is to drive ever better performance and the right behaviours through encouragement and development. We are looking for leaders who can embody our core values of being admired (for their artistry) at the same time as being respected (for their pragmatic achievements). All our staff need to be able to exhibit creativity in tandem with absolute professionalism.

When we did psychometric testing among the senior partners using the Myers-Briggs Type Indicator (MBTI) assessment method we found that we were all different psychological types, which shows that you do need a range of thinking and working styles to make a successful team. We are all different in how we derive our energy. In a successful team you need a good mix of doers, communicators and leaders.

What are your goals in architecture, and have they changed over the course of your career?

It is about having a real impact. I don't think my goals have really changed over time. I guess it is also about leaving a lasting legacy. Seeing the London A–Z with the full King's Cross scheme in place is something I really look forward to.

From your experiences, what do you think clients really want?

From my point of view as a client, I want the architect to really understand the full depth of the brief and to respond to it in as creative a way as possible. How can they do it better; not differently, but better? Some architects fall into the trap of believing that design leadership is about producing what they want to see. However, we are a pretty educated and knowledgeable client. We want the best ideas from our architects, but we don't want to be seen as just a vehicle for them to realise their own aspirations. Our architects need to make a difference that adds value to the project, not just their portfolio.

From your experiences, what do you think contractors really want?

Primarily the contractor wants clarity and certainty. They also value decisiveness. We get our best results when they are engaged early in the design process, certainly before the planning application stage. The contractor gets a better understanding of the project, earlier decision-making and greater certainty, and we benefit from them feeling a greater sense of ownership and more buy-in to the mutual aspirations and early advice from the supply chain.

Some years ago we had a project for a four-storey office building on a business park in the Thames Valley. Sidell Gibson Partnership was the architect and the contractor was part of what has now become BAM. There was a £250k Client Design Contingency, and we said that if at the end of the project it hasn't been spent the whole team can share it between them, but they have to stick to the overall cost target. During the project the architect and contractor came to us together and said that they wanted us to spend £50k of the contingency on improving the reception area, because they thought that what was proposed at the time didn't offer the right quality they wanted for the finished job and didn't reflect the standards they wanted to demonstrate. We said, '… but you'll lose the £50k.' That didn't deter them. It goes to show how things can work out if you do engender that sense of shared ownership.

What do architects really want?

Architects want to change the world for the better. I am sure that like everyone else they want to feel appreciated. Sometimes architects can be seen to be a bit too proud and arrogant, but this is probably just because they are essentially vulnerable, and care deeply. They do need to recognise that they are always going to be part of a wider team.

What is the main motivator that keeps you going?

There is so much left to do and so little time left to do it. I wake up in the morning and go to one of our offices located in one of the urban centres where we are working and I feel incredibly energised. I still want to be part of making buildings and places, something tangible and permanent. In the end I wouldn't feel the same about making anything more ephemeral, like an app or something. I don't think there is a property development app yet. You do need to relax sometimes as well, though. That is important.

What we do is about creating value. There is an element of disproving the traditional stereotypes about property developers; the fat cigars and the camel hair coats and all that. We are interested in creating social and cultural value as well as financial returns. It isn't a zero-sum game. We are also incredibly excited by good architecture. Inevitably the resources available to us are finite, but we can still make something fantastic. We want to leave a legacy, not just a good balance sheet.

Who has been most influential in helping you to achieve your professional goals and ambitions?

Somewhat scarily, my own MBTI personality type turns out to be the same as that of Ayn Rand, the author of *The Fountainhead*, the classic tale of the idealistic and individualistic architect who refuses to compromise his creative vision. There are a lot of architects that I admire. When I look at the work of Bob Allies and Graham Morrison, Alan Stanton and Paul Williams, Simon Allford, Dimitri Porphyrios, I just think, 'Wow, these architects are really on top of their game.' I imagine that at first for many of the architects we work with having an architect as a client can be the source of a bit of anxiety. They probably worry that I just want to use them to impose my design vision ahead of mutual goals, but that isn't how it works at all; it's collaborative.

If you could add one thing to the architectural education curriculum, what would it be?

Design is absolutely the core skill for architects, but I would add something on management. Not bean-counting, but an understanding of how to organise and use resources, and how an architect should manage their own business performance. Something on influencing and persuading as well: what does it take to be effective in explaining your ideas?

I think that architects do need to be given an understanding that there are a huge number of other stakeholders involved in the development process and given the opportunity to develop the skills to navigate this. They have to appreciate that these stakeholders all have legitimate needs. Perhaps there has been a little bit too much focus on the *starchitects*, although of course they don't achieve such success without having that understanding of the context in which they work. A more naive student might think it is just about wowing the client into submission, but the architect needs to find out what the client wants and then work out the best way to achieve that. The architect has to engage with the process; they can't be an aloof aesthete.

What knowledge, skills and capabilities do you look for in selecting architects?

They have to be able to demonstrate the attitude and capability to be effective within a team. I am looking for architects that have an opinion, are creative and inspiring, but at the

The ultimate inspiration – Falling Water

same time can be enough of a team player to get it delivered within the resource envelope and the other myriad constraints and influences.

What are the most important issues that will affect the business of architecture over the next decade?

Architects are going to increasingly be bidding and competing for work as members of teams; developers, contractors, designers, asset managers all coming together to deliver. The concept of whole life will come more to the fore. This is not just about whole life costs, but also embraces environmental and social sustainability. It is concerned with the complete range of resources: money, water, electricity, people.

I think that the future for cities is bright. Cities are where resources, people and ideas come together in one unique place.

Advances in computerisation will continue to change the way in which we handle information in the development process. We are already some way along the BIM pathway and there is further to travel.

Should more architects become developers?

They might want to give it a go ... but only they can decide. It might be great for some, but it has its own challenges. Perhaps it depends where they are on that artistic/pragmatic spectrum. Best of luck to them all in whichever path they choose!

11 SHANKARI RAJ EDGAR
NUDGE GROUP

Shankari Raj Edgar (Shanks) is an architect and educator based in Bristol. As well as tutoring at the Welsh School of Architecture and the University of the West of England (UWE), she is the founder and director of the multi-disciplinary design consultancy Nudge Group.

The innovative business model that Shanks has developed is focused primarily on community-led design, taking into account political, economic, social and architectural attributes of sites and locations, and providing services that embrace signage, branding, marketing and digital media in addition to more traditional architectural delivery. Much of the work of the practice has been in the provision of temporary spaces and installations. Currently Nudge is working on a scheme to provide facilities for over 60 start-up businesses and a public exhibition area in the Grade-I listed Brunel's Engine Shed adjacent to Bristol Temple Meads station.

For Shanks, undertaking work that adds social value is a prime driver. She talks about the importance of being able to relate to diverse groups of users and to really understand their needs, and explains the centrality of effective brief-making to her practice model. In recruiting their architectural staff, Nudge actively seek people with creative interests beyond architecture, and Shanks believes this is part of what gives the practice its dynamism and unique character.

During the interview, Shanks speaks about her desire to see more architects getting involved in political activity and influencing the urban planning agenda. She talks about the inspirational role politically engaged architects such as Jaime Lerner and George Ferguson have played in helping her to develop her own philosophy. Shanks feels that the culture of architectural education should embrace more generally the notion that there are many potential roles for architects beyond the narrow confines of traditional definitions of professional practice.

Shanks also speaks very honestly about the real financial, commercial pressures faced by contemporary architects and the challenges these pose to the profession.

Why did you become an architect?

I always ask my students this question. At school I was good at maths and I have always been very artistic. When I was around 17 years old, I did two periods of work experience, one in an aeronautical engineering business in Canada and the other with the graphic design visualisation and animation studio Three Blind Mice in London. Neither setting seemed quite right for me, though. I gravitated towards architecture as a natural balance between my analytical and design skills. My father wrote a number of books on technical drawing techniques, so I guess there was some background there.

What has been the single most rewarding experience in your career so far?

Seeing the smile on people's faces when you successfully deliver a vision for them is very rewarding. Many clients struggle to visualise from conventional architectural drawings and representations, so the best moment is often when they see an actual building or space for the first time. With many of our projects the greatest reward has been seeing people using and enjoying the spaces we have created for them. It is a fantastic feeling when you have fulfilled a creative vision through to pragmatic real delivery on the ground.

Which skill has been the most important for you in achieving success?

For me the most fundamental thing is being a people person, being genuinely interested in listening to people and getting to understand their needs. You have to have the ability to read between the lines of what people are saying. In our area of work the client can often in reality be a group of 20 or more people. Encapsulating all the different requirements and ideas in a unified vision can be a real challenge, but it is also very rewarding and is a key element of the architect's skill set. It is a kind of socio-politics. These skills aren't always developed in the schools of architecture. We aren't always shown how to be interested in what and how our clients think.

What has been the most significant lesson you have learned from a mistake or something that went wrong on a project?

On every project there are a lot of little things that you worry about but you can usually work them out. Budgets are constantly under pressure and you frequently have to make minor adjustments to your direction without losing sight of your vision and goals. The key thing in avoiding major problems is effective communication. You also need to have the foresight to be able to see potential difficulties before they arise.

At Nudge we have worked on a number of projects where we have done the master planning, or taken the project to a planning application, and then the project management for the delivery stages has been led by others. This hasn't always had a positive impact; it very much depends on the individual project manager. Perhaps we ought to hold on to the project management as often as we can, but I am not sure that I want to always be the project manager because my core skills are in design. Should you be prepared to relinquish some control or should you lead everything from beginning to end? It is a really difficult dilemma.

There is a lot of innovation in what we do at Nudge. Lots of our schemes are for temporary usage. Many of our projects are very community focused and we are very concerned with social value. You certainly need the right project manager for these types of project.

What do you feel have been the hardest barriers to overcome in achieving your success, and how have you dealt with them?

As a practice, it is the chicken and egg situation in relation to finding work. To get the larger projects you pretty much have to be a larger practice, but I am not that interested in being a bigger size of business. The flexibility of being smaller and being a collective, of being able to take on board the right additional individuals on a project-by-project basis, is part of what gives us our unique quality. If you are running a big engine that has to pay lots of people's mortgages, then you have a different set of restrictions to contend with. We don't have an interest in doing jobs that have no social value associated with them, and my fear is that if you grow too much then you'll end up having to take on work that doesn't match your values just to keep up your turnover.

We get most of our projects through the relationships we develop with individual people and networks. I think we do fairly unique work. Often we are effectively part of the client collective, and we generally have clients who share our values, and that is why they want to work with us.

In identifying future leaders in your business, what characteristics and qualities do you look for?

When I interview people I look for charisma, energy, the ability to be a team player and also having passions beyond and in addition to architecture. We recently took on someone who is also a musician and will be working for us three days per week for the next year or so. We have a Part 2 assistant who is hugely into ceramics. I believe that having people with different interests brings greater dynamism to your team.

We also want staff members that are nice people. By which I mean people who are honest and fair, who can listen and have got time for others.

What are your goals in architecture, and have they changed over the course of your career?

You have to question what success means. For many people success is about money, the size of your practice and fame. It is based on a very traditional model of the economy. I have been thinking a lot about what direction to take. At heart my goals revolve around the desire to create great places for people, but the bigger picture for Nudge is still constantly developing. We take things forward project by project. We want to find clients who share our values. We need to believe in a project in order to be able to do our very best work. Personally, I want to do socially useful things. A lot of the work of Nudge is community led and really quite political. Jaime Lerner and George Ferguson are great examples of how architects can become politically engaged to great effect. The whole area of urban planning is certainly one we would like to explore more in the future.

From your experiences, what do you think clients really want?

The design has to meet the budget or you lose credibility. It has to meet the brief. Often the client is unsure or unclear about the brief, so we usually formalise a very detailed document that everyone can sign up to. Achieving consensus on an accurate brief is critical to a successful outcome. In order to satisfy expectations everyone has to be clear from the outset about what is going to be delivered. This process of brief-making is a vital skill for the architect and an area where we can really add value.

From your experiences, what do you think contractors really want?

The reality is that the main concern for most contractors is the financial return. There are some who have a more nuanced approach, but they seem to be the exceptions, not the rule. As the designer you need to get a grip on the project budget from the very beginning and deliver to it. If not, you are inevitably going to be engaged in some difficult value engineering.

What do architects really want?

For me it is making a practical difference to people's lives, and I believe that design is absolutely able to deliver that.

The collective profession is probably really no different to any other professional group. Some people want money, some want recognition. There are many different types of architectural personality so you can't really generalise. I suppose you hope that all architects have some style!

What is the main motivator that keeps you going?

Everyone says I have a lot of energy. Working together with my friends and getting to see them every day is a plus. Having the pleasure of working with some really great clients is my main motivator.

Who has been most influential in helping you to achieve your professional goals and ambitions?

I would have to say my mum and dad, for all their support and encouragement throughout my education and in setting up our practice, and my husband. My friends and colleagues have always been very influential.

George Ferguson has been the architect who has inspired me the most. He can think very strategically and has nurtured projects throughout Bristol that have really brought new life to places and transformed lives.

If you could add one thing to the architectural education curriculum, what would it be?

That's easy: getting students to interact more with some real clients and to do more making of things. I think we should also be educating our students of architecture to be politicians as well as architects. Just having career politicians isn't healthy for a democracy. Architects are well placed to play a role in balancing economic and social sustainability more coherently.

What knowledge, skills and capabilities do you look for in newly qualified architects?

They need a strong CV that shows a range of interests and skills. Obviously, they need to be strong in design; this needs to come across in their portfolio. It doesn't matter what medium it is presented in. It is the quality of the space-making that I am looking for. I am looking for a demonstration of a command of both form and function.

What advice would you give to a newly qualified architect looking to make their way in the profession?

I think we should think of an architecture degree as more like a geography degree. It isn't a sign of failure if you study architecture and don't follow a lifelong career as a professional architect in the strict traditional definition of the role. The core skills of analysis and design can be applied in a wide variety of fields. So I would say to the newly qualified don't be confined by narrow definitions of what it is to be an architect. The more architects who enter into different types of private and public sector organisations, the better it will be for our society.

You do need to be self-analytical and recognise what you are best at and where your weaknesses lie. Architecture is a very broad subject and architects can't necessarily excel at every aspect. If you aren't really good with people then perhaps there are other areas on which you can focus. If your skills are in the resolution of technical problems then that might be an area in which to specialise. You have to value the skills you have.

What are the most important issues that will affect the business of architecture over the next decade?

Contractors and sub-contractors are eroding the design role of the architect. Quantity surveyors tend to dominate project management roles. So many people think that they can do what architects do. These are really big challenges for the architecture profession. To a large extent these developments have been all too predictable for some considerable time, and as a profession we have largely failed to respond.

I think that we will need to be more innovative. At Nudge we are trying to do some things differently partly because the wider systems in which we operate have changed. In the USA an ever increasing proportion of people are self-employed. We are certainly giving our staff as much flexibility as possible to operate in multiple dimensions. Women in particular can benefit from more adaptable and flexible working patterns. The idea of a nine-to-five job in a fixed location is not necessarily going to work anymore.

There is a strong streak of the social entrepreneur in me. For example, at the moment I am very interested in festivals. There is a lot of energy and drive deployed in setting them up, but it is frequently dissipated at the end of the event and there is often little lasting imprint. We are currently working to explore ways in which temporary installations at festivals and events can leave more of a legacy – socially, culturally and economically.

New technologies are clearly going to have a major impact on the future of architectural practice. There are some really practical benefits with BIM, for example, all of which are really useful, particularly when it comes to coordinating technical information and clash detection. However, my own view is that people should stay away from BIM in the early project stages because I think it narrows design thinking and inhibits creativity.

Redcliffe Wharf, Bristol. A proposal to spark Bristol's imagination. A new public space for the city delivered through a community share offer

12 SORAYA KHAN

Patrick Theis and Soraya Khan founded Theis + Khan in 1995. Originally based in the creative metropolitan powerhouse of Shoreditch, the practice relocated more recently to the leafier surroundings of Tunbridge Wells. They have produced a number of award-winning schemes, including their radical redesign of the 1960s Lumen Church in Bloomsbury, with its mix of spaces for quiet contemplation and lively community interaction, and their robust, finely crafted and highly contextual Bateman's Row mixed-use development in Shoreditch, which was shortlisted for the prestigious RIBA Stirling Prize in 2010.

Theis + Khan describe their approach as one of humanism in architecture that is characterised by an intense analysis of the purpose and siting of the building. The practice has demonstrated great adaptability and dexterity by completing an impressively varied portfolio of projects, encompassing churches and community centres, nurseries, offices, shops, mixed-use buildings, art galleries, health centres, housing developments and one-off private houses.

Soraya describes how the process of understanding and interpreting a client's needs, their ways of living and working, their likes and preferences, and the brief-making that this informs, are central to her method of creating architecture. She explains that while her end goal is always to make successful and beautiful buildings and spaces, her best projects are those in which the clients have found the design and construction process itself a fulfilling, creative and memorable experience, ones in which the collaborative journey has been integral to the delivery of an end result that has fully met the client's needs and exceeded their expectations. These are the projects that are most rewarding for the dedicated and committed architect.

In her interview, Soraya talks about some of the practical, commercial and psychological challenges that architects face, and about the need to sometimes recognise your own limitations and seek out the people with the complementary skills you need. She also identifies the need to develop business and communication skills if you are to survive and prosper as a successful and viable architectural practice and to create the space to design and deliver high-quality architecture.

Why did you become an architect?
Physical spaces have always fascinated me. As a little girl, I could appreciate spaces; I wanted to shape and feel them. That led to an interest in creating spaces; I really loved playing with Lego.

I was brought up in Hampstead, and an early home was a flat in a Norman Shaw building. I remember there was a stained-glass window that really attracted my attention. There was a lion or a similar animal, but it was the colours and the light coming through the glass that made the staircase landing space so magical to me.

Later on I used to borrow the *Daily Mail Book of House Plans* from the local lending library, and I began to show an interest in architecture. I remember going on a visit to an architectural office. A friend of my dad arranged it for me, I think. It was a large council architects' department. They showed me around the office and the work on the drawing boards, and I immediately thought I want to do this, I can do this.

What has been the single most rewarding experience in your career so far?

The most rewarding experiences come when you revisit a building with a client and they show you the bits that they are enjoying, that are really working for them. I get a great feeling when I go back to the Lumen Church and I see the local people using the community spaces and just hanging out in the café.

Which skill has been the most important for you in achieving success?

For me, it is probably the ability to understand and interpret a client's needs. From there you follow through to the whole design and delivery process. If you don't get the development of the brief right then you can't succeed. You have to have listening skills. You do have to interview the client, to tease it out of them. The client doesn't always understand what it is that you need from them. How they work, how they operate, what they like about their existing building, what they don't want – these are all important pieces of the puzzle.

We would never start by saying what you should do is this. It is listening first and asking the right question to get responses to build up the brief.

It can be a challenge if you have a client who doesn't respond, one who doesn't have a particular view. Once we had a really bad client meeting in which we presented a scheme that was met with total silence. That really was pretty awful, a quite devastating experience, but it has only happened to us once.

What has been the most significant lesson you have learned from a mistake or something that went wrong on a project?

Creating architecture is a complex process and you inevitably make many mistakes. It is a mistake not to respond to an instinctive feeling that a project is not going quite right; you need to pick up on that intuition and rethink if you are on the right track. The most important thing is to learn from your errors. Experience teaches you all the time, and you shouldn't make the same mistake twice. Definitely the biggest lesson that I have learned is to rely on your instincts, your gut feeling, whatever you like to call it.

What do you feel have been the hardest barriers to overcome in achieving your success, and how have you dealt with them?

The hardest barriers are those within oneself – your own shortcomings. Most external barriers can be overcome, but you also have to get beyond your own weaknesses. This is partly about learning when to bring in people with the skills you may lack. That is why architecture is such a team game. Sometimes your own internal barriers are just psychological. Working together in partnership has been important for us in this regard. Patrick and I draw immense strength from each other.

In identifying future leaders in your business, what characteristics and qualities do you look for?

An appreciation and understanding of our practice's work and approach is very important. Alongside that we look for enthusiasm, flexibility, determination. We look for people with a will to see the practice succeed, which is perhaps another way of saying being a good team player. We are looking for people who share our ambitions. It may sound corny, but it is like being part of a family. If you don't share the family values then possibly you will never quite fit in.

We are such a difficult couple in some ways. In our practice, the people who have worked most successfully with us are those that have really understood how Patrick and I work together. They also understand our shortcomings and enjoy enhancing our skills as a team.

We have a humanist approach to design, rather than an ideological, theoretically driven methodology. We aren't pretentious. Our focus is on the client and we adapt to the needs of the people on each project.

What are your goals in architecture, and have they changed over the course of your career?

My goals haven't really changed over time. I want to design successful buildings. You don't go into architecture to make money; it's a vocation. First and foremost, I would define a successful building project as one with a happy client. Hopefully it is also a beautiful building. Making something that is both beautiful and works for people is the greatest pleasure. People from all walks of life do recognise and appreciate beauty in the built environment.

From your experiences, what do you think clients really want?

A building and spaces that enable them to live and work better, that enhance their lives practically and spiritually.

Clients go into building projects knowing that there will be some hassle, but they do enjoy it as well. We want it to be a fulfilling experience for our clients. For many clients it may be the first and only time that they take on something of this kind, and it can be a very creative and memorable experience for them. We want the client to feel positive about the process, the journey, as well as the result. A while ago we worked with a number of bankers on their private houses. It was an unusual and rewarding experience for them to be able to get deeply involved with something aesthetically creative.

From your experiences, what do you think contractors really want?

Contractors do want to make a profit; that is without doubt their first priority. I would say that good contractors also enjoy the process of producing the finished building. Good contractors want to work well with the rest of the team. That really is the difference with the better contractors. On our part, we want to get the contractor involved, to ask their opinions, to benefit from their knowledge and experience, to include them in a creative way. It is an important means of helping them to feel ownership and a part of the creative team and process.

What do architects really want?

Architects want to create successful, beautiful buildings. The urge to make wonderful spaces is visceral for architects. There is plenty of hassle attached to doing building projects; architecture certainly isn't an easy profession. Why do we do it? That urge, desire really, to create the very best buildings and spaces is very strong.

What is the main motivator that keeps you going?

For me it is all about the creative process. It isn't really about making money or pleasing our peers, but we do care very much about earning the approval of our clients.

Who has been most influential in helping you to achieve your professional goals and ambitions?

For myself, I think I always need a patron figure. That started with parental support and interest. Then it was the support of my tutors at college – that was really important to my development. In practice you need the interest of the client. In a way, it is the same kind of relationship at different stages in your evolution as an architect. It is vital for me to have someone who is interested in me and my work. It is the artist–patron relationship. It does feel very necessary to the whole process.

Your relationships with your peers do give you an indication of your position in the architectural world, but that doesn't directly impact upon the work.

If you could add one thing to the architectural education curriculum, what would it be?

I would have to say business skills, no question. I do recognise the necessity for architects to have better business skills. Although money is far from the main driver for architects, you do need to keep afloat financially. One of the most important people in our practice is our office manager. Having a great office manager enables us to focus our time and effort on the core stuff, but you do need to understand the business aspects. Architectural projects also involve large sums of money, and you have to be up to the task of managing that.

What knowledge, skills and capabilities do you look for in newly qualified architects?

In no particular order: common sense, curiosity, an ability to work in a team, self-possession, a sense of duty and responsibility to the practice and our clients.

The absolute basics are excellent drawing skills and design appreciation. Not all architects will be top designers – you don't necessarily need to be a brilliant designer in order to find your niche and succeed, but you can't support the process of creating architecture without an appreciation of what makes good design. That is essential. It is not all about being the star designer. You can still be a successful member of our team.

What advice would you give to a newly qualified architect looking to make their way in the profession?

Pick up as much knowledge as possible about absolutely everything. You do need to be a bit of a know-all and to make yourself as valuable as possible.

At the same time, it is also useful to hone a particular skill or expertise that a practice may need. Don't be wishy-washy about it – find something that can make you uniquely valuable to your practice. A practice won't want to drop someone who has got something special and of value to offer. It is an extremely competitive professional environment in architecture, and you have to stand out.

I think that enthusiasm also goes a long way.

What are the most important issues that will affect the business of architecture over the next decade?

Communicating the value of good design is the big challenge for the architecture profession. What is it that makes a building into architecture and why does that matter? We need to make it clear that good design is affordable; it just takes a little time and thought.

In my experience, when clients do get the value of design, they really get it, so it is vital for us to be able to put it across. There is a real financial return as well; it translates into better design outcomes and higher fees.

I could set out a great long list of all the other issues facing us, but for me this is the paramount concern. It is a very complicated thing to tackle, but extremely important. Architects will be chasing a relatively small and diminishing pool of work if we don't effectively and successfully demonstrate the value that we add.

Our latest church project 'Watford URC'

'Sir Christopher Wren
Said, "I am going to dine with some men.
If anyone calls
Say I am designing St. Paul's." '[4]

04__Edward Clerihew Bentley, "Sir Christopher Wren" from *The Complete Clerihews* (Kelly Bray, Cornwall: House of Stratus, 2008). Reproduced with permission of the Curtis Brown Group Ltd., London, on behalf of the Estate of E C Bentley. Copyright © the Beneficiaries of the Literary Estate of E C Bentley 1905.